Sulphide
Marbles

Stanley A. Block & M. Edwin Payne

4880 Lower Valley Road, Atglen, PA 19310 USA

Dedication

This book is dedicated to all of the craftsmen who produced these gems and to my family, from whom the hobby has taken so much time.

Stanley A. Block

This book is dedicated to my wife Joni and my three daughters, Melissa, Robin, and Holly, who spent many hours cramped up in the car accompanying me to various marble meets and auctions around the country over the past seventeen years. They helped make those long drives seem so much shorter. They also have a keen set of eyes for good marbles.

M. Edwin Payne

Library of Congress Cataloging-in-Publication Data

Block, Stanley A.
Sulphide marbles / Stanley A. Block, M. Edwin Payne.
p. cm.
ISBN 0-7643-1340-1
1. Sulphides (Art)--Collectors and collecting--Catalogs. 2. Marbles (Game)--Collectors and collecting--Catalogs. I. Payne, M. Edwin. II. Title
NK5440.S8 B58 2001
748.8--dc21
2001000405

Designed by Bonnie M. Hensley
Cover design by Bruce M. Waters
Type set in Zapf Humanist Dm BT/Souvenir Lt BT

ISBN: 0-7643-1340-1
Printed in China
1 2 3 4

Published by Schiffer Publishing Ltd.
4880 Lower Valley Road
Atglen, PA 19310
Phone: (610) 593-1777; Fax: (610) 593-2002
E-mail: Schifferbk@aol.com
Please visit our web site catalog at **www.schifferbooks.com**

In Europe, Schiffer books are distributed by Bushwood Books
6 Marksbury Avenue Kew Gardens
Surrey TW9 4JF England
Phone: 44 (0) 20-8392-8585; Fax: 44 (0) 20-8392-9876
E-mail: Bushwd@aol.com
Free postage in the UK. Europe: air mail at cost.

This book may be purchased from the publisher.
Include $3.95 for shipping. Please try your bookstore first.
We are always looking for people to write books on new and related subjects.
If you have an idea for a book please contact us at the above address.
You may write for a free catalog.

Contents

Acknowledgments

We would like to thank Ed Payne, who actually got this project started. He gave us the impetus to build on his efforts.

We would also like to thank Bob Block for his help at the start of this project.

Our sincere thanks to all of the collectors who have allowed us the opportunity to see and photograph their treasures. Their generosity has allowed us to build a very substantial photo library, which has helped to round out the contents of this book. It is our hope this book will help to promote the marbles hobby, the Marble Collectors Society of America, and especially sulphide marbles.

Once again, I would be remiss if I did not thank my family for any undue hardships caused by my time spent with the society and its projects, and for their help in completing some of them. Thank you all.

Stanley A. Block
Chairman

Marble Collectors Society of America

The Marble Collectors Society of America was founded in 1975 as a non-profit organization, established for charitable, scientific, literary, and educational purposes. The Society's objectives are to gather and disseminate information and perform services to further the hobby of marbles, marble collecting, and the preservation of the history of marbles and marble making. The Society currently has over 2,000 contributors.

Society projects include the quarterly newsletter, *Marble Mania*®, color marble photograph plates, a videotape series, and contributor's listings. In addition, we are in the process of ongoing research and development for the Society library, along with development of a collection of marbles for the Society library, which will be available on a loan basis to libraries and museums.

Other major accomplishments of the Society to date are the uninterrupted issuance of a quarterly newsletter, *Marble Mania*®*;* various surveys; photographing and publishing color sheets; gathering and placing collections in museums (The Smithsonian, The Corning Museum of Glass, and the Wheaton Village Museum); publication of price guides, with periodic updates; work toward establishing a library of articles and marble related materials;

preparation of slide presentations; preparation and publication of contributor listings; research and issuance of articles concerning marble factories and contemporary marble makers; publication of Mark Randall's booklet, *Marbles as Historical Artifacts;* preparation of videotapes on marbles, including the first two-hour videotape on collecting marbles; and classification and appraisal services; as well as the book *Marble Mania*®, and Robert Block's book *Marbles: Identification and Price Guide*. In addition to the above, the Society is working on additional table top books covering all facets of the hobby of marbles. These books will expand on the book *Marble Mania*® which was published in 1998.

Each book will be a photographic manual, covering a specific section of the hobby. Each book is planned to contain over 500 photographs. The first of these expanded books, *Contemporary Marbles* by Mark Block, was published in October 2000. It contains over 800 photographs representing well over 100 glass artisans.

This book on sulphide marbles contains over 600 photographs and is the first of three books planned to cover antique, handmade glass marbles.

Introduction

History

A sulphide marble is a solid glass sphere containing a clay-type figure. Sulphide marbles can trace their lineage directly back to the sulphide cameos and bas-reliefs which were encrusted in glass in England, France, and Central Europe in the early nineteenth century.

Unlike all other handmade glass marbles, the process for making a sulphide marble consists of fusing two disparate substances (glass and clay) together, in a manner such that the encrustation (the sulphide figure) is perfectly visible from the outside of the marble. In order to produce glass encrusted objects, it became necessary to find a substance that could fuse with the glass. The encrusted object had to be capable of being heated to a temperature higher than the glass, exhibit the property of not expanding or contracting as it was heated and cooled, and be capable of exhausting minimal amounts of gas as it was encrusted in the hot glass. This presented tremendous technical challenges to glassmakers, and the process was only perfected during the nineteenth century.

By the seventeenth and eighteenth centuries, glass workers had experimented with encasing various materials in glass. Early examples exist of glasses containing dice or coins. The oldest glass containing a die, "v Ni Kostka Zadelana," is included in a 1584 inventory of the collection of Lady Johanna Trzka von Leipa, which was in the archives in Wittingau (Jokelson 12). The dice were usually bone, an organic material which could not be worked into red-hot glass. So, the die were probably enclosed into the glass using a cold process, "Zwischengoldtechnik" (Jokelson, 12). Cold process objects were placed in a hollow of glass and the opening or entry point was sealed. There are also somewhat later glasses that include metal coins. These were probably made using a hot process at the glassworks. However, not all of the coins were solidly secured within the glass, so, they change position and can rattle.

It has been reported that around 1750 a Bohemian manufacturer experimented with encasing small gray clay figures in glass (Pellat). However, it appears that there were numerous difficulties in producing acceptable figures and then creating the encrusted pieces. Few eighteenth century Bohemian pieces have survived. Little is known of Bohemian or German sulphide production prior to the 1820s. By that time, sulphide making and glass-encrusting had been perfected in France.

The process of encrusting Sulphides in glass was perfected in France around 1796. This process stemmed from the production of sulphide cameos and their use in jewelry and on china. One of the earliest French manufacturers of sulphide cameos was a father and son team with the surname of Deprez (their first names are not known). The elder Deprez is listed in the Paris Commercial Almanacs of various years between 1793 and 1813 as a producer of porcelain cameos. At the 1806 Paris Exhibition he was awarded the silver medal. There is no mention of glass encrustations, however it is known that porcelain cameos were used on china and in jewelry.

In 1818 Pierre Honore Boudon de Saint-Amans took out a patent for making flat sulphide medallions, and for perfecting the process of encrusting cameos in glass. This would indicate that there was an earlier patent granted for this process, although no mention can be found of that patent in the literature. During the Louvre Exhibition of 1819 Saint-Amans, who is not listed at the 1806 exhibition, is noted as a maker of encrusted Sulphides. Desprez [the son] appears at the exhibition only as the maker of porcelain cameos. However, in a Commercial Almanac issued after the Exhibition, Deprez (the son) appears as a maker of porcelain cameos in the Wedgwood style and with the description, "Assortement de Medailles dans l'interieur de cristal."

Prior to the 1819 Exhibition, Deprez (the son) received a patent for the porcelain sulphide he invented (from Nevers sand, white quartz, purified kaolin from Limoges, and earth from Dreux). By 1821, the Commercial Almanac lists Deprez solely for the encrustation of Sulphides in glass.

It has been stated that all of Desprez's Sulphides are conspicuous for their great precision, something which cannot be said for later French manufacturers (Jokelson). They have no air lines or air bubbles, only a silvery sheen caused by a thin film of air escaping from the slip and being sandwiched between the sulphide figure and the glass.

During the 1820s and 1830s, a number of manufacturers in Paris began producing a variety of glass encrusted sulphide items. These included glass, vases, jars, girandoles (wall mounted glass candleholders), jewelry and paper-weights. It is highly doubtful that the French ever produced sulphide marbles.

The art of sulphide-making spread across the Channel to England. By 1831, an Englishman, Apsley Pellatt, had secured a patent for producing "Crystallo-Ceramie." Pellat describes the process of creating a die of the sulphide, producing the sulphide figure and then creating the following, "ornaments of any description - coats of arms, ciphers, portraits and landscapes of any variety of colour - . . . enclosed within glass, so as to become chemically imperishable."

During the Napoleonic era, glass encrustations spread from France to Germany. It has been reported [Jokelson] that sulphide items were originally imported from France to be encrusted in glass. Potsdam-Zechlin Glass Works were probably the first manufacturers of encrusted glass Sulphides in Germany [Jokelson]. The most important piece is a polished egg-shaped vase in the Chateau on Peacock Island which - according to the inventory of 1835 - was given by the president of Zechlin Glass Works to King Frederick William III (who reigned from 1786 to 1797). Jokelson also reports that glass encrustation's were produced in Silesia, and in the area now known as the Czech Republic, in the 1820s and 1830s. By the late 1820s, the sulphide figures themselves were being produced in Germany. German glass encrustations were shown for the first time at the Prague Industrial Exhibition of 1829, and with such great success they received the Gold Medal. Production seems to have continued intermittently, with sulphide paperweights known to have been produced in this area as late as the 1920s.

Interestingly, French sulphide making seems to have been confined to busts, medallions, and allegorical "plaques." English sulphide making encompassed these subjects, as well as figures and hand painted Sulphides, predominantly scenes. German and Czech sulphide making included some of these items, but also plaques with transferred images.

The period of "high-art" French and English sulphide-making lasted only through the mid-nineteenth century. Inexplicably, this process then lapsed for a period of almost seventy-five years, until an American paperweight dealer, Paul Jokelson, convinced two of the French glass houses, St. Louis and Baccarat, to again produce sulphide paperweights (around 1951). Those two companies, plus a Scottish glass house called Pertshire, as well as several American glass houses (see Section V, Chapter 4) still produce sulphide paperweights. However, most glass collectors would agree that current sulphide-making in no way approaches the quality of nineteenth century French and English Sulphides.

Process

The creation of a sulphide marble is a multi-step process:

1. A mold of the sulphide figure is created. These molds are created much the same as molds for other cast items. A model is sculpted in clay or wax. Some models also exist that are carved in marble blocks. Depending on whether the sulphide is a plaque-type or a three-dimensional figure, a single sided mold or a mold of each side of the sculpture is created. The mold can be of plaster of paris, ceramic, or metal (iron molds have been reported).

2. The sulphide compound is mixed (generally clay, potash, and water) and poured into the mold. The slip is allowed to dry so that minimal moisture exists in it. The sulphide figure is then removed from the mold and seam marks are trimmed or ground off.

3. There are two different processes for encasing the sulphide figure into the glass. In each process, the sulphide figure is heated to a temperature comparable to the molten glass.

4. In one process (the blown method), a gather of glass is picked up on the end of a hollow metal tube (punty). The glassworker blows down the tube to create a hollow space in the glass gather. A second worker uses glass shears to snip open the end of the hollow gather. The pre-heated sulphide figure is then placed in the hollow opening of the gather and then the open end is pressed closed. The glassworker then sucks air out of the tube which causes the glass gather to collapse around the sulphide figure. The glassworker does not get burned by the hot air in the glass gather, because he is sucking the cool air out of the tube, which causes the hot air in the gather to rush out of the enclosed space, into the tube, and then atmospheric pressure closes the space. The glass marble is then reheated, rounded on a marver, and annealed, the same as any other handmade marble.

5. In the second process, the pre-heated sulphide is placed in a small container on any of a variety of stands. A small gather of molten glass is then poured over the sulphide to encase it. In older techniques, a small layer of glass is rubbed over the sulphide forcing air expelled by the sulphide to come out the back and not be trapped in the front. This technique is known as the weld method. More modern methods use a small vacuum device to suck air from the bottom of the container. This vacuum forces the gases released by the sulphide figure out the bottom of the container, preventing them from becoming trapped around the sulphide. The glass encrusted sulphide is picked up on a rod. It is then either encased in a thick outer layer of glass, to create the correctly sized marble, or it is simply re-heated, rounded, and annealed, just like any other handmade marble.

Artistry, Craft and Technical Skill

As you can see from this discussion of the process, great skill was needed to produce a sulphide. The original sculpture required a high level of technical skill to create.

Many of the busts and medallions were simply copied from paintings and drawings of the time. However, a number of the allegorical medallions and landscapes exhibit true artistry. Unfortunately, very few of the Sulphides in marbles exhibit artistry. Interestingly, while many of the Sulphides created for glassware and display objects were images of famous people, events, or scenes, almost all marble Sulphides were objects from common, everyday living in an agrarian based society: farm animals, pets, wildlife, common people, and religious images. Very few marble Sulphides were produced of famous people or symbols.

Once the sulphide figure was created, the encrustation of that sulphide required significant technical skill. In the instance of the blown method, the air had to be extracted from the pocket in a very controlled manner, or the figure would have a trapped air bubble on it. In the instance of the weld method, great care was needed when encrusting the sulphide figure, or air would be trapped either in front of or behind the figure.

You see many instances of trapped air bubbles in sulphide marbles. You rarely see such bubbles with other glass encrusted sulphide objects. Rather than this being simply a quality control issue, with defective encrusted glasswares being discarded while marbles were retained, this is probably the result of much greater care being employed in the production of glass encrusted sulphide objects than was taken when producing sulphide marbles. Certainly, sulphide marbles exist in far greater numbers than all other glass encrusted sulphide objects combined. Almost all sulphide marbles were produced as children's toys. The exceptions to this would probably be some of the marbles featuring either religious motifs or some of the more famous busts. By contrast, all glass encrusted sulphide objects were produced for sale to the middle and upper classes as decorative objects or jewelry.

Antique Sulphide Marbles

Antique sulphide marble making was practiced in Germany and in the United States. No evidence exists that sulphide marbles were made in France or England. While the date of the first sulphide marble is not known, it can be surmised that production probably started in the 1860s or 1870s. This is inferred because sulphide marbles exist with the following figures:
1. Memorial to James Garfield (featuring a wreath around him, with Chester Arthur on the reverse). He was assassinated in 1872.
2. Jenny Lind, The Swedish Nightingale. She was brought to the United States and popularized by P.T. Barnum in 1850 and into 1852.
3. General George A. Custer. The Battle of Little Big Horn was in 1876.
4. Christopher Columbus. The Columbian Exposition was in 1892.
5. Kaiser Wilhelm. He reigned from 1888 to 1918.

Interestingly, sulphide marbles exist of both Kaiser Wilhelm and American presidents. However, there are no known examples with Queen Victoria or any French political figures, lending credence to the assertion that sulphide marbles were not produced or even popular in those countries. Of course, since sulphide marbles were produced almost exclusively in Germany, English and French subjects might not have been produced for nationalistic reasons.

Sulphide marbles were produced predominately in Germany, with some reported to have been produced in early American glass houses (Iowa City Flint . . .).

There are no sulphide marbles known to exist that have the quality of sulphide that you find in French or English glass encrusted sulphide items. The quality of marble Sulphides is very similar to German/Czech paperweights. French and English Sulphides items were produced in small art-glass houses, German/American Sulphides were produced using techniques that would be considered mass-production at the time. French and English sulphide items were truly artistic items, or minimally fine craft. German/American Sulphides were almost exclusively produced as toys.

Antique Sulphides can be segmented into several subcategories:

1. Domestic Animals
2. Farm Animals
3. Wild Animals
4. Aquatic Animals
5. Birds and Fowl
6. Human Figures
7. Mythical or Allegorical Figures
8. Religious Figures
9. Inanimate Objects

Watch What You Buy

Most marble collectors and dealers are the nicest people you will ever meet. Most of the dealers were or are collectors. As in all collectible fields, marble collecting has had its bad apples. Luckily, they have been few and far between.

There is nothing wrong with having a marble restored, if it will make it a more collectible example. Most collectors can tell a polished marble. Grinding and polishing removes the folds and creases in the surface, making them perfectly smooth. It is more difficult to find chips and holes that have been filled. Using a 10x power glass and a black light (most marble dealers carry them), check the surface. Usually under black light, a filled hole will stick out like a sore thumb. In addition, some marbles that are damaged are being coated with a space age coating that makes the marble look as though it is in mint condition. This is a service to collectors that turns a damaged rarity into a displayable example.

The problem occurs later when the marble changes hands. It might end up in the wrong hands and be resold without qualification. The best way to check is to hold the marble in the palm of your hand. The coating acts as an insulator that causes the marble to feel warmer than one that has not been coated. There is also a different feel to the surface. Another way to tell is to take a pocket knife and scrape a small area. Scraping at the end of a marble won't do any damage. On an expensive marble, it is best to get a written guarantee.

Finally, some chipped or fractured marbles are being reheated. This process can be identified by checking the surface of the glass and the pontil area. It leaves a fire polished surface, losing the seams and folds normally found on the surface. Just take your time and pay attention to the details. If in doubt, get a second opinion.

Unless the price is extremely low, so that you cannot be hurt by a mistake, examine your potential purchase carefully. Know who you are buying from. Sellers should be willing to guarantee what they are selling for both type and condition. If purchasing through the mail, you should be extended a five or ten day return privilege. If purchasing at auction, you should read the terms and conditions of sale. Most regular auctions are 'as is, where is' without any guarantees or returns. Auctioneers who specialize in marbles usually guarantee type, size, and condition. Again, that will be stated in their terms and conditions.

The marble organizations, individual collectors, and dealers do try to police unfair practices and unscrupulous characters who periodically appear. Word does get around, and sooner or later that character gets the word and disappears. If you do have a bad experience, let other collectors and the organizations know about it. In some cases, guarantees were not asked for or given. In other cases, purchases were made at flea markets or shows, after which the seller is gone and cannot be reached. These bad deals become valuable learning experiences. Almost every collector has had at least one such experience. Do not be embarrassed by bad experiences; learn from them.

Pictures and Listings

Listings of known sulphides have been developed and gathered over many years. Subjects have come from many sources including collectors, books, magazines and newspaper articles, for sale ads, auctions, and estate sales.

To cover the various types of sulphides and give them some sense of order, this book is broken down into groups including various types of animals, birds and fowl, aquatic animals, humans, religious, mythical, and inanimate objects. Within each group are examples of single, multiple, colored glass, and colored figure sulphide marbles. There are alphabetical listings for each group as well as a full alphabetic list of all currently known subjects.

These listings are by no means complete, as there are still new finds that are not on the list. We have included photos of as many examples as we could find, but have not been able to photograph every marble on the lists. We would have liked to do it, but time constraints and lack of knowledge of the location of owners of the missing examples prevented us from accomplishing that feat.

Except for ten or twelve rare subjects from the book *Marble Mania*, all other photos in this book have been taken during the past two years. Some of the marbles featuring various subjects displayed here may be the same as those in *Marble Mania*, but the examples shown here were all photographed specifically for this book.

There were times when the identification of certain subjects was difficult and open to individual interpretation. However, it was our goal to identify all subjects by their generally accepted terminology. In some cases, figures are known by two common names shown in parenthesis (for example Buffalo (Bison); Clown (Dunce, Jester); Moses in basket (Baby in a basket)).

Also, some figures look so much alike that two or three different names can be given to that figure (e.g., Otter, mink, marmot). In this instance, we have listed our assessment of the figure.

It should also be noted that, depending on the interpretation and identification, the same figure may belong in two different classifications (e.g., Boy (Leprechaun), humans/mythical; Old Man (Santa Claus), humans/mythical; Woman on a horse, humans/farm animal!).

In the above cases, the category that applies would be the one most commonly used. In the case of multiple figures, the more dominant valued category would be used (e.g., Woman on a horse – humans).

Alphabetic Listing of Known Sulphides
Antique Sulphide Marble Subjects

Note: Figures may be in a variety of positions which may not be noted below (i.e., standing, running, sitting, etc.).

- Afghan Hound
- Aire-wolf
- Alligator
- Alpaca
- Anteater
- Anchor
- Angel
- Angel Playing Flute
- Ape
- Ape Man
- Ape Man in Colonial Dress
- Armadillo
- Baboon
- Baby
- Baby in Basket
- Baby in Cradle
- Badger
- Bantam Rooster
- Barrister (Lawyer)
- Bat
- Bear
- Bear Holding Pole
- Bear with Bat
- Bear with Fish
- Bear with Hat
- Beaver
- Beethoven
- Bird
- Bison
- Boar
- Boy
- Boy Baseball Player
- Boy Carrying a Basket
- Boy in Sailor Suit with Boat
- Boy on Stump
- Boy Praying
- Boy with Accordion
- Boy with Dog
- Boy with Hammer
- Boy with Hat
- Boy with Horn
- Bride
- Buffalo
- Bull
- Bust of Beethoven
- Bust of Columbus
- Bust of Golithe
- Bust of Horses Head with Reigns and Flowing Mane
- Bust of Jenny Lind
- Bust of Woman
- Buzzard
- Calf
- Camel
- Cannon
- Caribou
- Cat
- Cellist
- Cheetah
- Cherub in a Blanket
- Cherub Head
- Cherub Head with Wings
- Chick
- Chicken
- Child with Book
- Child with Dog
- Child with Croquet
- Face of Child on Disc
- Child on Sled
- Chow Dog
- Christ on Cross
- Christopher Columbus
- Circus Bear
- Clown
- Cockatoo
- Coin
- Coin with Numbers
- Collie
- Colt
- Cow
- Cougar
- Court Jester

- Coyote
- Crane
- Crane Eating Fish
- Davy Crockett
- Crow
- Crucifix
- Dachshund
- Deer
- Demon
- Dik Dik
- Doe
- Dog
- Dog with Bird
- Dog with Duck in Mouth
- Dolly Madison
- Dove
- Donkey
- Dromedary (One Humped Camel)
- Drum
- Drummer Boy
- Duck
- Duck Flying
- Dunce
- Dutch Boy
- Eagle
- Eagle (Thunderbird Type)
- Eagle on Ball
- Eagle with Arrows in Claws
- Elephant
- Elf
- Elf with Wings
- Egret
- Emu
- Face on a Disc
- Falcon
- Fish
- Flower
- Flying Goose
- Flying Owl
- Fox
- Franz Josef
- Frog
- Gargoyle
- George Washington Full Figure in Uniform
- Gengis Khan Head
- Girl
- Girl Bathing
- Girl Brushing Hair
- Girl Sitting in Swing
- Girl Sitting on a Wall
- Girl with Doll
- Girl with Mallet & Ball
- Girl Praying
- Gnome
- Goat
- Goose
- Gorilla
- Grouse
- Harps Eagle
- Half Dime
- Hawk
- Hedgehog
- Hen
- Hippo
- Hog
- Honey Bee
- Horse
- Horse with Saddle
- Hunter Carrying Deer
- Hyena
- Iguana
- Initial
- Jackal
- Jenny Lind
- Kaiser Wilhelm
- Kangaroo
- Kate Greenway
- Kitten, Face Only
- Lamb
- Leopard
- Leprechan
- Lion
- Lioness
- Little Boy Blue
- Little Red Riding Hood
- Lizard
- Llama
- Lobster
- Lobster on Rock
- Love Birds
- Madonna
- Madonna Seated on a Throne
- Mandolin Player
- Mandrill
- Man Holding Hat
- Man on Horse
- Man on Potty
- Man with Rifle
- Marmot
- Mary Gregory
- Mermaid
- Mink
- Monkey
- Monkey with Banana
- Monkey with Hat on Head
- Monkey with Wings
- Moses in a Basket
- Mother Goose
- Mountain Goat
- Mouse
- Mule
- Mummy
- Newt

- Nude Boy
- Nude Girl
- Numbers 0-9
- Numbers 10-13
- Numbers on Shields or Coins 0-10
- Otter
- Owl
- Owl Man (Coat with Tails)
- Pan, Mythical Character
- Panda
- Papoose
- Panther
- Parrot
- Partridge Standing
- Peacock
- Peasant
- Pegasus (Flying Horse)
- Pelican
- Penguin
- Penny
- Pheasant
- Phoenix Bird
- Pig
- Pigeon
- Pocket Watch
- Polar Bear
- Pomeranian
- Pony
- Porcupine
- Presidents
- Prospector
- Puma
- Punch & Judy
- Puss 'N' Boots
- Quail
- Quarter Dollar (1858)
- Quasimodo (Hunch Back of Notre Dame)
- Queen Victoria
- Rabbit
- Rabbit Reading a Book
- Raccoon
- Ram
- Ram's Head
- Rat
- Revolutionary War Soldier
- Rhinoceros
- Rocking Horse
- Robin
- Teddy Roosevelt
- Rooster
- St. Bernard
- Sailing Ship
- Santa Claus
- Santa on Potty
- Scoter (Water Bird)
- Seagull
- Seal
- Sea Lion
- Shark

- Sheep
- Ship with Masts
- Snake
- Snail
- Soldier
- Sparrow
- Sphinx
- Squirrel
- Stags Head
- Stage Coach
- Stork
- Sturgeon
- Swan
- Sword
- Teddy Bear
- Tiger
- Tigress
- Tin Man
- Totem Pole Eagle
- Train
- Troubadour
- Turkey
- Turtle
- Vulture
- George Washington
- Weasel
- Whale
- Whippet (Dog)
- Wicked Witch
- Wolf
- Wolf with Shawl (from Red Riding Hood?)
- Wolverine
- Women with Basket
- Woodcock
- Woman
- Woman - Face on Disc
- Woman Sitting on Potty
- Woman with Basket
- Woman with Dog

Colored Glass

- Angel (Deep Purple)
- Baby in Basket (Blue)
- Bear Holding Trunk (Amber) (Blue)
- Beaver (Green)
- Bird (Green)
- Boar (Amber)
- Buffalo (Deep Purple)
- Camel (Amber)
- Cat (Cobalt) (Amber)
- Cat on Platform (Blue)
- Child (Green) (Amber) (Blue)
- Chicken (Amber)
- Clown (Cobalt)
- Coin #2 (Purple)
- Court Jester (Cobalt)
- Cow (Amber) (Blue)
- Crane (Blue)

- Dog (Amber) (Blue) (Amethyst)
- Eagle (Green) (Amber)
- Eagle (Light Green) (Teal Blue)
- Elephant (Purple) (Blue)
- Elf (Blue)
- Fish (Amethyst)
- Frog (Amber)
- Horse (Cobalt) on Rock (Aqua) (Green)
- Hyena (Green)
- Lamb (Green) (Cobalt)
- Leprechaun (Blue) (Green)
- Lion (Amber) (Blue)
- Lion (Green) Brown Mane and Black Eyes
- Lioness (Amber)
- Love Birds, a pair (Aqua)
- Man Carrying Sack (Green)
- Man in Thought on Rock (Aqua)
- Mandolin Player (Green)
- Monkey (Amber)
- Moses in Basket (Blue)
- #1 (Green)
- #2 (Cobalt)
- #5 (Coin Type) (Purple) (Green)
- #6 (Green)
- #8 (Coin Type) (Green)
- #3, #4 (Blue)
- Panther (Amber)
- Pig (Amber) (Green)
- Pigeon on Stump (Blue Glass) (Amethyst)
- Rabbit (Amber)
- Ram (Amber)
- Rhinocerous (Blue)
- Rooster (Amber) (Blue) (Green) (Yellow)
- Sheep (Amber) (Green) (Amethyst) (Blue)
- Squirrel (Blue) (Green) (Amber) (Cobalt)
- Woman Standing (Amber) (Green)

Double Sided

- Bull's Head; Hunter with Gun and Rabbit
- Cat, two-faced
- Deer Head, Boy or Child with Goat
- President and Running Mate
- Squirrel Eating Nut; Ram Lying Down When Marble is Turned 180 Degrees

Two Subjects

- Chicken & Sheep
- Children Holding Hands
- Cow with Calf
- Double Eagle
- Double Madonna
- Girl with Lamb
- George Custer - on both sides
- Hen with Rooster on Top
- Hunter Carrying a Deer
- Little Boy Blue and Sheep
- Lizard and Worm (one on each side)

- Madonna with Girl Reading Book
- Pair Doves
- Pair Fish
- Pair Lovebirds
- Peasant Dancers (Man and Woman)
- Rooster and Dog
- Seated Boy and Girl
- Sheep with Lamb at Side
- Soldier with Musket and Spouse

Three Figures

- Bird, Cat, and Fish
- Three Bears
- Three Fish

Colored Figures

- Angel - Blue Trim on Wings
- Bear Holding Log (Figure is Brown)
- Bird - Blue Wings, Yellow Beak, on Green Stump
- Boy - Red Hair
- Bust of Jenny Lind - Green Dress
- Bust of Jenny Lind - Red Hair, Black Facial Features, Aqua Dress
- Cat - Green Ground, Black Spots, Tail and Facial Features
- Clown - Blue Hat, Black Facial Features
- Cow - Various Colors
- Dog - with Spots, Green Ground
- Dog - Brown Hat (Ears), Black Spots and Facial Feature on Green Ground
- Dog of Flanders - Dark Brown Coat, White Eyes with Black Pupils, Green Grass
- Fox - Brown Stripe, Head to Tail
- Hen - Various Colors
- Horse - Black Eyes, on Green Ground
- Horse - Black Eyes, Red Mane, Green Grass
- Horse - on Brown Mound, Black Facial Features, Blue Mane
- Jenny Lind - Blue Dress, Golden Hair
- Lamb on Green Ground, Black Facial Features
- Lion - Amber Mane
- Numbers in Blue (3, 4)
- Numbers on Shield (Blue)
- Number 1 - Blue Number on Odd Shaped White Metal
- Parrot - Four Colors
- Peacock - Three Colors
- Pigeon - Green Pedestal, Blue Wings, Black Beak
- Ram - Lying in Green Glass, Horn, Facial Features in Brown
- Rhino on a Green Ground
- Rooster - Blue Stripes on Feathers, Green Ground
- Squirrel - Brown on Green Grass
- Turtle - Purple Shell
- Weasel on a Green Ground

Section I: Animals

Domestic Animals

Cats and Dogs

Size	Mint	Near Mint	Good	Collectible
under 1"	$200.-	$150.-	$50.-	$30.-
1" to 1 3/16"	$150.-	$100.-	$50.-	$30.-
1 1/4" to 2"	$175.-	$100.-	$50.-	$30.-
over 2"	$250.-	$150.-	$50.-	$30.-

Premiums For:

Unusual figures or special features such as donut holes or secondary items	1x to 10x
Unusual poses	1x to 5x
Multiple figures	3x to 25x
Painted figures or colored glass (but not light tints)	5x to 25x

Deductions For:

Buffed surface	10% to 20%
Off center (depending on degree)	20% to 40%
Ground and polished surface	20%
Annealing fractures or missing parts	20% to 50%
Trapped air bubbles that obscure view	20% to 40%

Examples

	Photo #'s	
Two sided cat's face	9 thru 12	3 to 6x chart above
Dog with duck in mouth	55 & 56	2 to 4x chart above
Colored figures	1, 13, 16, 20 thru 23, 35 & 36	8 x 15X chart above
Colored figures	33 & 34	20 to 25x chart above
Colored glass	5, 16, 24, 37 thru 39	10 to 20x chart above

I-1-1. Seated cat, black spots, tail, ears, and facial features, green ground, 1 1/4". *Courtesy of Stan Block.*

I-1-2. Seated cat, 1 1/2". *Courtesy of Stan Block.*

I-1-3. Seated cat, 1 1/2". *Courtesy of anonymous.*

I-1-4. Seated cat, 1 1/2". *Courtesy of anonymous.*

I-1-5. Seated cat, light brown glass, 1 1/8". *Courtesy of Jerry Biern.*

I-1-6. Seated cat, brown tongue, 1 3/4". *Courtesy of Stan Block.*

I-1-7. Reclining cat, 2". *Courtesy of Stan Block.*

I-1-8. Reclining cat, 2 1/4". *Courtesy of Block's Box.*

I-1-9. Two sided cat's face, front, 13/16". *Courtesy of Wilburn Powell.*

I-1-10. Two sided cat's face, back, 13/16". *Courtesy of Wilburn Powell.*

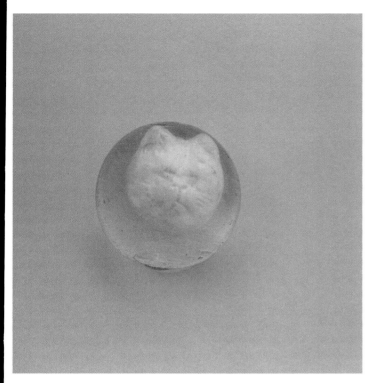

I-1-11. Two sided cat's face, front, 7/8". *Courtesy of Stan Block.*

I-1-12. Two sided cat's face, back, 7/8". *Courtesy of Stan Block.*

I-1-13. Begging dog, black ears and facial features, green ground, 1 3/8". *Courtesy of Jeff Yale.*

I-1-14. Begging dog, 1 1/8". *Courtesy of Stan Block.*

I-1-15. Begging dog, 2". *Courtesy of anonymous.*

I-1-16. Reclining dog, amber glass, 1 3/8". *Courtesy of Stan Block.*

I-1-17. Reclining dog, 1 1/8". *Courtesy of Stan Block.*

I-1-18. Reclining dog, 1 7/8". *Courtesy of anonymous.*

I-1-19. Reclining dog, 1 3/4". *Courtesy of Stan Block.*

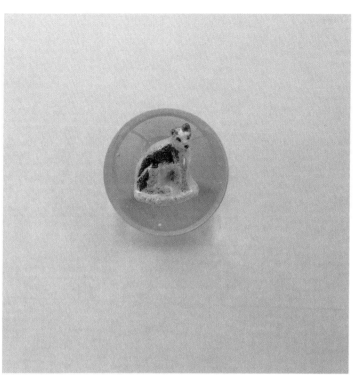

I-1-20. Dog seated on hind quarter, black spots, ears and facial features, 1 3/8". *Courtesy of Wilburn Powell.*

I-1-21. Dog seated on hind quarter, reverse of above (I-1-20), 1 3/8". *Courtesy of Wilburn Powell.*

I-1-22. Dog seated on hind quarter, black spots, eyes, ears, and facial features, green ground, 1 1/2". *Courtesy of Stan Block.*

I-1-23. Dog seated on hind quarter, reverse of above (I-1-22), 1 1/2". *Courtesy of Stan Block.*

I-1-24. Dog seated on hind quarter, amber glass, 1 1/8". *Courtesy of Stan Block.*

I-1-25. Dog seated on hind quarter, 1 5/8". *Courtesy of anonymous.*

I-1-26. Dog seated on hind quarter, collie, 1 3/4". *Courtesy of Jerry Biern.*

I-1-27. Dog seated on hind quarter, collie, 1 3/4". *Courtesy of Stan Block.*

I-1-28. Dog seated on hind quarter, 1 3/4". *Courtesy of anonymous.*

I-1-29. Dog seated on hind quarter, 1". *Courtesy of anonymous.*

I-1-30. Dog seated on hind quarter, 1 3/8". *Courtesy of Marble Collectors' Society.*

I-1-31. Dog seated on hind quarter, greyhound, 1 7/8". *Courtesy of Stan Block.*

I-1-32. Dog seated on hind quarter, brown body, white eyes, green ground, 2". *Courtesy of Stan Block.*

I-1-33. Standing dog, Dog of Flanders, 2". *Courtesy of Art & Donna Clayton.*

I-1-34. Standing dog, Dog of Flanders, 2". *Courtesy of Art & Donna Clayton.*

I-1-35. Standing dog, brown/black spots, green ground, 1 7/8". *Courtesy of Jerry Biern.*

I-1-36. Standing dog, reverse of I-1-35, 1 7/8". *Courtesy of Jerry Biern.*

I-1-37. Standing dog, amber glass, donut hole under belly, 1 3/8". *Courtesy of Jerry Biern.*

I-1-38. Standing dog, purple glass, 1 5/8". *Courtesy of Block's Box.*

I-1-39. Standing dog, amethyst glass, 2". *Courtesy of Wilburn Powell.*

I-1-40. Standing dog, tail up, 1 1/8". *Courtesy of Stan Block.*

I-1-41. Standing dog, tail up, 1 5/8". *Courtesy of Stan Block.*

I-1-42. Standing dog, Chow, tail up, 1 1/4". *Courtesy of Stan Block.*

I-1-43. Standing dog, tail up, 1 3/4". *Courtesy of Stan Block.*

I-1-44. Standing dog, tail down, 1 1/2". *Courtesy of Stan Block.*

I-1-45. Standing dog, tail down, 1 1/2". *Courtesy of Stan Block.*

I-1-46. Standing dog, tail down, reverse of I-1-45, 1 1/2". *Courtesy of Stan Block.*

I-1-47. Standing dog, tail down, 1 3/4". *Courtesy of anonymous.*

I-1-48. Standing dog, tail down, 1 1/2". *Courtesy of anonymous.*

I-1-49. Standing dog, tail down, reverse of I-1-48, 1 1/2". *Courtesy of anonymous.*

I-1-50. Standing dog, tail down, 1 3/4". *Courtesy of Jerry Biern.*

I-1-51. Standing dog, tail down, reverse of I-1-50, 1 3/4". *Courtesy of Jerry Biern.*

I-1-52. Standing dog, tail down, 2 1/8". *Courtesy of Scott Strasburger.*

I-1-53. Standing dog, tail straight, 1 3/8". *Courtesy of Scott Strasburger.*

I-1-54. Standing dog, tail straight, 1 1/2". *Courtesy of Stan Block.*

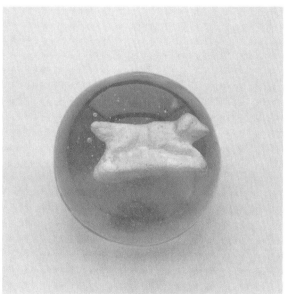

I-1-55. Dog w/ duck in mouth, 1 1/2". *Courtesy of Ed Payne.*

I-1-56. Dog w/ duck in mouth, front view of I-1-55, 1 1/2". *Courtesy of Ed Payne.*

Farm Animals

Alpaca	Horse
Calf	Llama
Cow	Pig
Donkey	Ram
Goat	Sheep

Size	Mint	Near Mint	Good	Collectible
under 1"	$200.-	$150.-	$50.-	$30.-
1" to 1 3/16"	$150.-	$100.-	$50.-	$30.-
1 1/4" to 2"	$175.-	$100.-	$50.-	$30.-
over 2"	$250.-	$150.-	$50.-	$30.-

Premiums For:

Unusual figures or special features such as donut holes or secondary items	1x to 10x
Unusual poses	1x to 5x
Multiple figures	3x to 25x
Painted figures or colored glass (but not light tints)	5x to 25x

Deductions For:

Buffed surface	10% to 20%
Off center (depending on degree)	20% to 40%
Ground and polished surface	20%
Annealing fractures or missing parts	20% to 50%
Trapped air bubbles that obscure view	20% to 40%

Examples

	Photo #'s	
Unusual Poses	16, 21, 22, 38, 53*, 54	3 to 6x chart above
Rare figure	46	8 to 15x chart above
Colored figures	9, 10, 11, 30, 31, 43, 44	8 to 15x chart above
Colored glass	12, 25, 26, 33, 45 thru 50, 55 thru 58	10 to 15x chart above
Two figures	64	15 to 25x chart above

*Photo 53 also has an amethyst tint. Add 10% to the total.

I-2-1. Alpaca, 2". *Courtesy of Stan Block.*

I-2-2. Calf, 1 1/2". *Courtesy of Stan Block.*

I-2-3. Cow, 2 1/4". *Courtesy of Stan Block.*

I-2-4. Cow, reverse of I-2-3, 2 1/4". *Courtesy of Stan Block.*

I-2-5. Cow, 1 1/2". *Courtesy of Stan Block.*

I-2-6. Cow, 1 3/4". *Courtesy of anonymous.*

I-2-7. Cow, 1 7/8". *Courtesy of anonymous.*

I-2-8. Cow, reverse of I-2-7, 1 7/8". *Courtesy of anonymous.*

I-2-9. Cow, brown/black spots and facial features, green ground, 2". *Courtesy of Hansel DeSousa.*

I-2-10. Cow, black spots and facial features, green ground, 1 3/8". *Courtesy of Stan Block.*

I-2-11. Cow, reverse of I-2-10, 1 3/8". *Courtesy of Stan Block.*

I-2-12. Cow, blue glass, 1 3/4". *Courtesy of Jeff Yale.*

I-2-13. Donkey (mule), 1 5/8". *Courtesy of Stan Block.*

I-2-14. Donkey (mule), 1 3/4". *Courtesy of Stan Block.*

I-2-15. Donkey (mule), 1 7/8". *Courtesy of Jeff Yale.*

I-2-16. Goat, note two donut holes, 1 7/8". *Courtesy of Jeff Yale.*

I-2-17. Goat, 1 3/4". *Courtesy of Stan Block.*

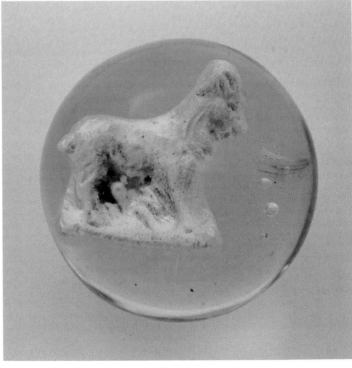

I-2-18. Goat, reverse of I-2-17, 1 3/4". *Courtesy of Stan Block.*

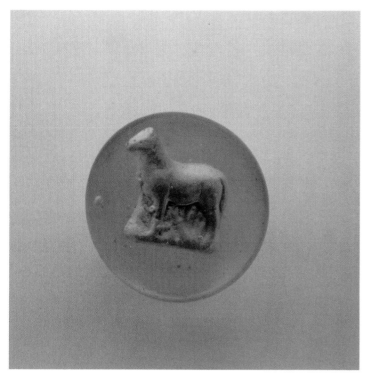

I-2-19. Horse, standing, 1 5/8". *Courtesy of Stan Block.*

I-2-20. Horse, standing, 1 5/8". *Courtesy of Stan Block .*

I-2-21. Horse, standing with saddle, 2 1/4". *Courtesy of Stan Block.*

I-2-22. Horse, standing with saddle, 1 5/8". *Courtesy of Stan Block.*

I-2-23. Horse, horse feeding, donut hole, 1 5/8". *Courtesy of anonymous.*

I-2-24. Horse, horse feeding, donut hole, 1 3/4". *Courtesy of Jerry Biern.*

I-2-25. Horse, running horse in green glass, 1 1/4". *Courtesy of Jerry Biern.*

I-2-26. Horse, running horse in green glass, 1 3/8". *Courtesy of Jeff Yale.*

I-2-27. Horse, running horse, 1 7/8". *Courtesy of Stan Block.*

I-2-28. Horse, horse rearing, 1 5/8". *Courtesy of anonymous.*

I-2-29. Horse, horse rearing, 1 3/4". *Courtesy of Bob Pommrehn.*

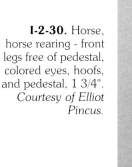

I-2-30. Horse, horse rearing - front legs free of pedestal, colored eyes, hoofs, and pedestal, 1 3/4". *Courtesy of Elliot Pincus.*

I-2-31. Horse, reverse of I-2-30, 1 3/4". *Courtesy of Elliot Pincus.*

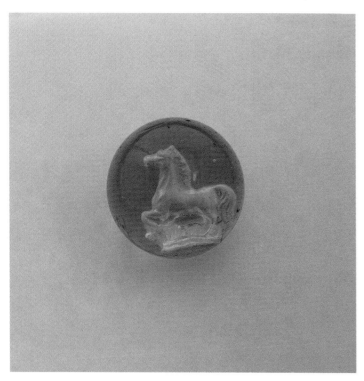

I-2-32. Horse, horse rearing - donut hole, 1 3/4". *Courtesy of Wilburn Powell.*

I-2-33. Horse (pony), standing - tinted amber glass, 1 7/8". *Courtesy of Stan Block.*

I-2-34. Horse (pony), running pony, 1 1/2". *Courtesy of Stan Block.*

I-2-35. Horse (pony), running pony, 1 1/4". *Courtesy of anonymous.*

I-2-36. Horse (pony), running pony, 1 3/8". *Courtesy of anonymous.*

I-2-37. Horse (pony), rearing pony, 1 1/2". *Courtesy of Stan Block.*

I-2-38. Llama, standing, 2 1/4". *Courtesy of Stan Block.*

I-2-39. Pig, 2 1/2". *Courtesy of Stan Block.*

I-2-40. Pig, 1 3/8". *Courtesy of anonymous.*

I-2-41. Pig, to show size of the actual sulphide and magnification due to the curvature of the glass, 1 3/8". *Courtesy of Stan Block.*

I-2-42. Pig, (reverse of I-2-41), 1 3/8". *Courtesy of Stan Block.*

I-2-43. Ram, standing colored figure, 1 3/4". *Courtesy of Stan Block.*

I-2-44. Ram, reclining colored figure, 1 1/4". *Courtesy of Stan Block.*

I-2-45. Ram, blue tinted glass, 1 7/8". *Courtesy of Stan Block.*

I-2-46. Ram, head only, 1 3/4". *Courtesy of Stan Block.*

I-2-47. Sheep, amber glass, 1 3/8". *Courtesy of Wilburn Powell.*

I-2-48. Sheep, amethyst tinted glass, 1 3/4". *Courtesy of Stan Block.*

I-2-49. Sheep, green tinted glass, 1 3/4". *Courtesy of Stan block.*

I-2-50. Sheep, green tinted glass, 2 3/8". *Courtesy of Block's Box.*

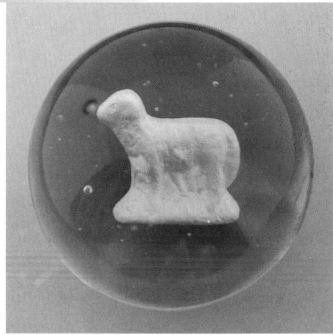

I-2-51. Sheep, 1 1/2". *Courtesy of Stan Block.*

I-2-52. Sheep, 2 1/8". *Courtesy of anonymous.*

I-2-53. Sheep, with a lamb - amethyst tint, 1 3/4". *Courtesy of Stan Block.*

I-2-54. Sheep, with a lamb, 1 5/8". *Courtesy of Block's Box.*

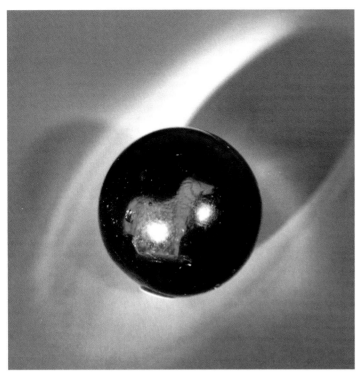

I-2-55. Sheep (lamb), cobalt blue glass, 1 3/8". *Courtesy of Jeff Yale.*

I-2-56. Sheep (lamb), green glass, 1 5/8". *Courtesy of Stan Block.*

I-2-57. Sheep (lamb), amber glass, 1 3/8". *Courtesy of Stan Block.*

I-2-58. Sheep (lamb), amethyst glass, 2 1/8". *Courtesy of Jeff Yale.*

I-2-59. Sheep (lamb), rear leg scratching ear, 1 1/2". *Courtesy of Stan Block.*

43

Wild Animals

Ape	Deer	Hyena	Panther	Squirrel
Bear	Dik Dik	Lion	Porcupine	Wolf
Boar	Elephant	Lioness	Rabbit	Wolverine
Buffalo	Fox	Monkey	Rat	
Camel	Gorilla	Mountain Goat	Rhinoceros	

Size	Mint	Near Mint	Good	Collectible
under 1"	$200.-	$150.-	$50.-	$30.-
1" to 1 3/16"	$150.-	$100.-	$50.-	$30.-
1 1/4" to 2"	$175.-	$100.-	$50.-	$30.-
over 2"	$250.-	$150.-	$50.-	$30.-

Premiums For:

Unusual figures or special features such as donut holes or secondary items	1x to 10x
Unusual poses	1x to 5x
Multiple figures	3x to 25x
Painted figures or colored glass (but not light tints)	5x to 25x

Deductions For:

Buffed surface	10% to 20%
Off center (depending on degree)	20% to 40%
Ground and polished surface	20%
Annealing fractures or missing parts	20% to 50%
Trapped air bubbles that obscure view	20% to 40%

Examples	Photo #'s	
Unusual Figures	15, 16, 19, 20, 30, 31, 51, 69, 74, 76, 79, 81, 82, 103, 104, 112, 113	3 to 6x chart above
Colored Figures	12, 61, 122	8 to 15x chart above
Colored glass	3, 8, 14, 16, 46, 53, 62, 68, 72, 73, 77, 114, 115, 123	10 to 15x chart above
Two Figures	21, 22, 105, 106	15 to 25x chart above

I-3-2. Ape, 2". *Courtesy of Stan Block.*

I-3-3. Ape Man, amethyst glass, 1 5/8". *Courtesy of Wilburn Powell.*

I-3-1. Ape, 2 3/8". *Courtesy of Bill Sweet.*

I-3-4. Bear, seated, 1 1/2". *Courtesy of Stan Block.*

44

I-3-5. Bear, seated, 1 1/2". *Courtesy of Stan Block.*

I-3-6. Bear, seated, 2 1/8". *Courtesy of Jeff Yale.*

I-3-7. Bear, seated, amethyst glass, 1 3/4". *Courtesy of Jerry Biern.*

I-3-8. Bear, seated in blue glass, 2". *Courtesy of Wayne Sanders.*

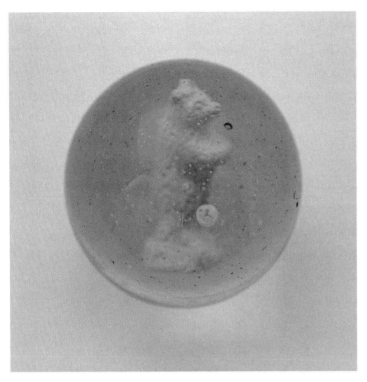

I-3-9. Bear, standing on hind legs, 1 5/8". *Courtesy of Stan Block.*

I-3-10. Bear, standing on hind legs, 1 7/8". *Courtesy of anonymous.*

I-3-11. Bear, standing on hind legs, holding a ball, 1 1/2". *Courtesy of Stan Block.*

I-3-12. Bear, standing on hind legs, brown figure, 1 1/2". *Courtesy of Jeff Yale.*

I-3-13. Bear, standing on hind legs, holding a pole, 1 1/4".
Courtesy of Marble Collectors Society.

I-3-14. Bear, standing on hind legs, holding a pole, amber glass
with a clear overlay, 1 1/2". *Courtesy of Elliot Pincus.*

I-3-15. Bear, standing on hind legs, holding a fish, 1 5/8". *Courtesy of Stan Block.*

I-3-16. Bear, amber glass, standing on hind legs, holding a pole, 1
1/2". *Courtesy of Wilburn Powell.*

I-3-17. Bear, begging, 1 1/4". *Courtesy of Stan Block.*

I-3-18. Bear, begging, 1 1/4". *Courtesy of anonymous.*

I-3-19. Circus bear, holding a log on back of head, 1 1/2".
Courtesy of Jerry Biern.

I-3-20. Circus bear, holding a log on back of head, 1 1/4".
Courtesy of Jeff Yale.

I-3-21. Bear, two bears - side view, 1 3/4". *Courtesy of Jerry Biern.*

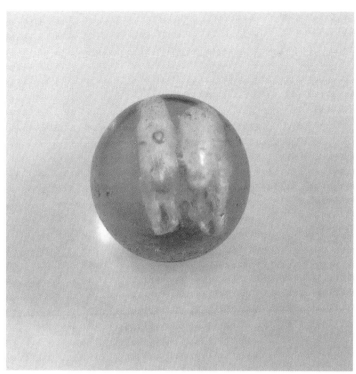

I-3-22 . Bear, two bears - top view, 1 3/4". *Courtesy of Jerry Biern.*

I-3-23. Bear, standing on all fours, 2". *Courtesy of Marble Collectors' Society.*

I-3-24. Bear, standing on all fours, 1 5/8". *Courtesy of anonymous.*

I-3-25. Bear, standing on all fours - polar bear, 1 5/8". *Courtesy of Stan Block.*

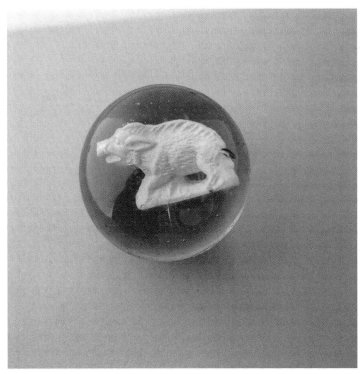

I-3-26. Boar, wart hog type, 2 1/8". *Courtesy of Elliot Pincus.*

I-3-27. Boar, reverse of I-3-26, 2 1/8". *Courtesy of Elliot Pincus.*

I-3-28. Boar, 2 1/16". *Courtesy of Bill Sweet.*

I-3-29. Boar, 1 3/8". *Courtesy of anonymous.*

I-3-30. Buffalo, 1 7/8". *Courtesy of Jeff Yale.*

I-3-31. Buffalo, 1 5/8". *Courtesy of Stan Block.*

I-3-32. Camel (dromedary), one hump, 1 3/4". *Courtesy of Wilburn Powell.*

I-3-33. Camel, one hump, 1 1/2". *Courtesy of Stan Block.*

I-3-34. Camel, one hump, 2 1/4". *Courtesy of anonymous.*

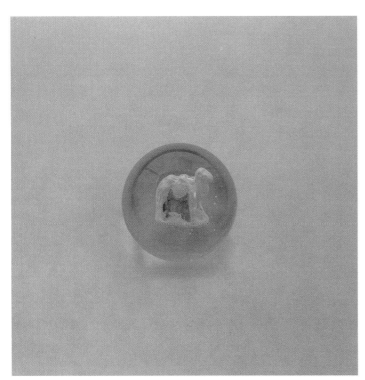

I-3-35. Camel, two humps, 1 3/8". *Courtesy of Wilburn Powell.*

I-3-36. Deer, standing, biting back, 1 1/2". *Courtesy of Stan Block.*

I-3-37. Deer, standing, 1 3/4". *Courtesy of anonymous.*

I-3-38. Deer, running, 1 3/4". *Courtesy of Stan Block.*

I-3-39. Deer, running, 1 1/2". *Courtesy of anonymous.*

I-3-40. Deer (doe), 2 1/4". *Courtesy of Jeff Yale.*

I-3-41. Dik-dik, 2". *Courtesy of Jerry Biern.*

I-3-42. Dik-dik, 1 1/2". *Courtesy of Hansel de Sousa.*

I-3-43. Elephant, 2". *Courtesy of Stan Block.*

I-3-44. Elephant, donut hole, 1 5/8". *Courtesy of Scott Strasburger.*

I-3-45. Elephant, donut hole, 2". *Courtesy of Wilburn Powell.*

I-3-46. Elephant, donut hole, blue glass, 1 1/2". *Courtesy of Jeff Yale.*

I-3-47. Fox, 1 1/2". *Courtesy of Stan Block.*

I-3-48. Fox, 1 1/2". *Courtesy of anonymous.*

I-3-49. Fox, 1 1/2". *Courtesy of Jeff Yale.*

I-3-50. Gorilla, 2 1/8". *Courtesy of Stan Block.*

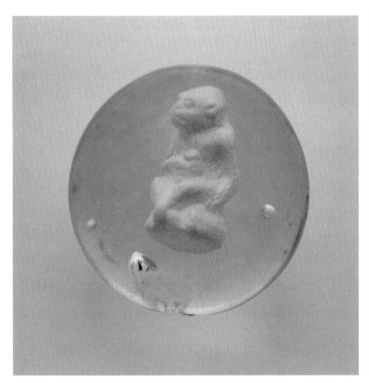

I-3-51. Gorilla, holding a baby gorilla, 1 1/4". *Courtesy of Stan Block.*

I-3-52. Hyena, 1 3/4". *Courtesy of anonymous.*

I-3-53. Hyena, in green glass, 1 3/8". *Courtesy of Stan Block.*

I-3-54. Lion, donut hole, 1 7/8". *Courtesy of Bernie Benavidez.*

I-3-55. Lion, 1 1/4". *Courtesy of anonymous.*

I-3-56. Lion, 2". *Courtesy of anonymous.*

I-3-57. Lion, 2 1/8". *Courtesy of Stan Block.*

I-3-58. Lion, 2". *Courtesy of Jerry Biern.*

I-3-59. Lion, 1 7/8". *Courtesy of anonymous.*

I-3-60. Lion, donut hole, 1 3/8". *Courtesy of Stan Block.*

I-3-62. Lion, amber glass, 1 1/2". *Courtesy of Wilburn Powell.*

I-3-61. Lion, painted figure, 2 1/8". *Courtesy of Jerry Biern.*

I-3-63. Lion, crouching, 2 1/8". *Courtesy of Block's Box.*

I-3-64. Lion, reclining, 1 7/8". *Courtesy of Trudy Christian.*

I-3-65. Lion, reclining, 1 3/4". *Courtesy of Stan Block.*

I-3-66. Lion, 1 5/8". *Courtesy of anonymous.*

I-3-67. Lion, 1 1/4". *Courtesy of anonymous.*

I-3-68. Lion, peacock blue glass, 1 3/8". *Courtesy of Stan Block.*

60

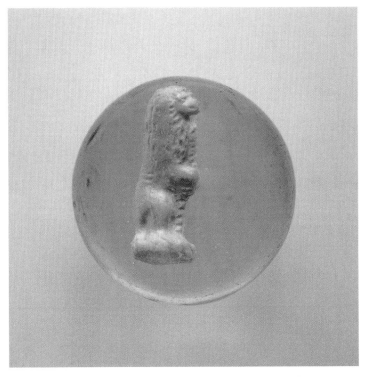

I-3-69. Lion, holding a pole, 2". *Courtesy of Stan Block.*

I-3-70. Lioness, 1 5/8". *Courtesy of Stan Block.*

I-3-71. Lioness, 2". *Courtesy of Jerry Biern.*

I-3-72. Lioness, donut hole, amber glass, 1 1/2". *Courtesy of Stan Block.*

I-3-73. Lioness, amethyst glass, 1 7/8". *Courtesy of Wilburn Powell.*

I-3-74. Monkey, organ grinder monkey with collar, 1 1/2". *Courtesy of Jeff Yale.*

I-3-75. Monkey, 2". *Courtesy of Jeff Yale.*

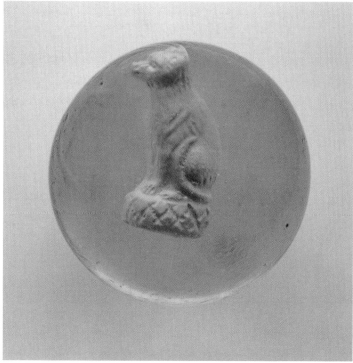

I-3-76. Monkey, seated on a drum, 2". *Courtesy of Stan Block.*

I-3-77. Monkey, amber yellow glass, 1 3/4". *Courtesy of Wayne Sanders.*

I-3-78. Monkey, 2 1/16". *Courtesy of Jerry Biern.*

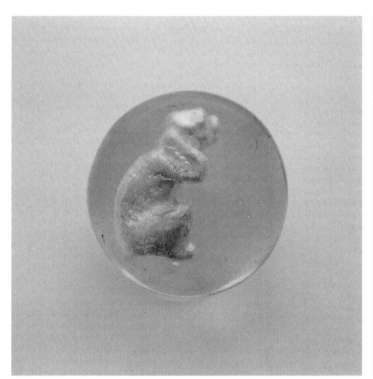

I-3-79. Monkey, scratching back of head, 1 1/4". *Courtesy of Stan Block.*

I-3-80. Mountain goat, 1 3/8". *Courtesy of Stan Block.*

I-3-81. Panther, 2 1/8". *Courtesy of anonymous.*

I-3-82. Panther, 1 1/2". *Courtesy of Block's Box.*

I-3-83. Porcupine, 1 1/4". *Courtesy of Stan Block.*

I-3-84. Porcupine, 1 1/2". *Courtesy of Stan Block.*

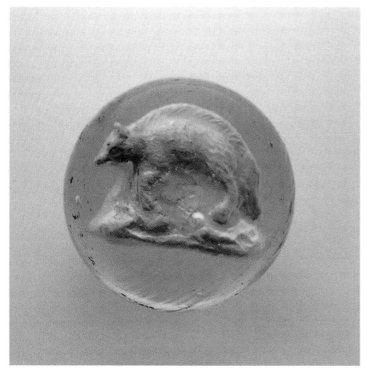

I-3-85. Porcupine, 1 5/8". *Courtesy of anonymous.*

I-3-86. Rabbit, 1 3/8". *Courtesy of anonymous.*

I-3-87. Rabbit, 15/16". *Courtesy of Stan Block.*

I-3-88. Rabbit, 1 3/8". *Courtesy of Jeff Yale.*

I-3-89. Rabbit, 1 1/2". *Courtesy of Stan Block.*

I-3-90. Rabbit, 1 1/2". *Courtesy of anonymous.*

I-3-91. Rabbit, 1 1/2". *Courtesy of anonymous.*

I-3-92. Rabbit, missing ears, 1 1/2". *Courtesy of Stan Block.*

I-3-93. Rabbit, 1 1/2". *Courtesy of Stan Block.*

I-3-94. Rabbit, 1 1/4". *Courtesy of anonymous.*

I-3-95. Rabbit, 1 3/4". *Courtesy of anonymous.*

I-3-96. Rabbit, 1 1/8". *Courtesy of Stan Block.*

I-3-97. Rabbit, 1". *Courtesy of Stan Block.*

I-3-98. Rabbit, 1 5/8". *Courtesy of Stan Block.*

I-3-99 . Rabbit, 1". *Courtesy of anonymous.*

I-3-100. Rabbit, 1 1/4". *Courtesy of Jerry Biern.*

I-3-101. Rabbit, 1 1/8". *Courtesy of Stan Block.*

I-3-102. Rabbit, 2". *Courtesy of anonymous.*

I-3-103. Rabbit, leaning against a stump, 1 7/16". *Courtesy of Jeff Yale.*

I-3-104. Rabbit, in coat reading a book, 1 5/8". *Courtesy of Jerry Biern.*

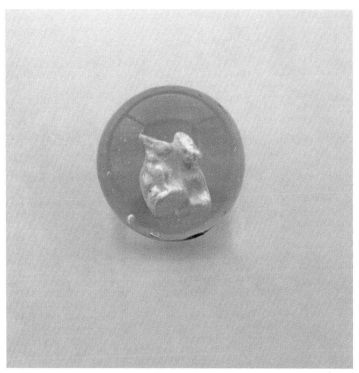

I-3-105. Rabbit, pair of rabbits, 1 5/8". *Courtesy of Wilburn Powell.*

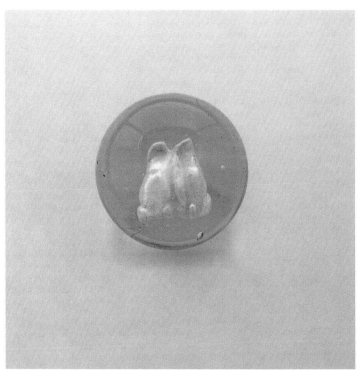

I-3-106. Rabbit, pair of rabbits - reverse of I-3-105, 1 5/8". *Courtesy of Wilburn Powell.*

I-3-107. Rat (mouse), 1 1/8". *Courtesy of Stan Block.*

I-3-108. Rat (mouse), 1 1/4". *Courtesy of Jeff Yale.*

I-3-109. Rat (mouse), 1 1/4". *Courtesy of Stan Block.*

I-3-110. Rat (mouse), 1 3/8". *Courtesy of Jeff Yale.*

I-3-111. Rat (mouse), wearing a hat, 1 1/4". *Courtesy of Stan Block.*

I-3-112. Rhinoceros, 1 7/8". *Courtesy of Jerry Biern.*

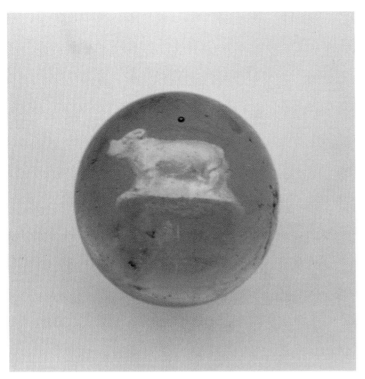

I-3-113. Rhinoceros, 1 3/4". *Courtesy of Stan Block.*

I-3-114. Rhinoceros, blue glass, 1 3/4". *Courtesy of Hansel de Sousa.*

I-3-115. Rhinoceros, blue glass, 1 1/2". *Courtesy of Jerry Biern.*

I-3-116. Squirrel,. 1 1/4". *Courtesy of Stan Block.*

I-3-117. Squirrel, front, 2 1/8". *Courtesy of Stan Block.*

I-3-118. Squirrel, side, 2 1/8". *Courtesy of Stan Block.*

I-3-119. Squirrel, 2 1/8". *Courtesy of anonymous.*

I-3-120. Squirrel, 1 1/2". *Courtesy of anonymous.*

I-3-121. Squirrel, 1 1/4". *Courtesy of Stan Block.*

I-3-122. Squirrel, brown figure, green base, 1 1/4". *Courtesy of Jerry Biern.*

I-3-123. Squirrel, green glass, 1 5/8". *Courtesy of Jerry Biern.*

I-3-124. Squirrel, 1". *Courtesy of anonymous.*

I-3-125. Squirrel, 1 1/4". *Courtesy of anonymous.*

74

I-3-126. Squirrel, eating a nut, 1 1/2". *Courtesy of Jeff Yale.*

I-3-127. Squirrel, held on side it looks like a ram, 1 1/2". *Courtesy of Jeff Yale.*

I-3-128. Squirrel, without a tail it's a begging bear, 1". *Courtesy of Stan Block.*

I-3-129. Wolf, 2". *Courtesy of Stan Block.*

I-3-130. Wolverine, 2". *Courtesy of Jerry Biern.*

I-3-131. Wolverine, 1 1/2". *Courtesy of Stan Block.*

Aquatic Animals

Beaver   Otter
Fish   Sea Lion
Frog   Seal
Iguana   Snail
Lizard   Turtle
Lobster   Whale
Newt   Worm

Size	Mint	Near Mint	Good	Collectible
under 1"	$300.-	$200.-	$100.-	$50.-
1" to 1 3/16"	$300.-	$200.-	$100.-	$50.-
1 1/4" to 2"	$300.-	$200.-	$100.-	$50.-
over 2"	$400.-	$300.-	$100.-	$50.-

Premiums For:

Unusual figures or special features such as donut holes or secondary items	1x to 10x
Unusual poses	1x to 5x
Multiple figures	3x to 25x
Painted figures or colored glass (but not light tints)	5x to 25x

Deductions For:

Buffed surface	10% to 20%
Off center (depending on degree)	20% to 40%
Ground and polished surface	20%
Annealing fractures or missing parts	20% to 50%
Trapped air bubbles that obscure view	20% to 40%

Examples

	Photo #'s	
Unusual Figures	4, 11, 12, 13, 15, 16, 17, 22, 23, 27, 29, 30	3 to 10x chart above
Colored Figures	26	5x chart above
Colored glass	32	10 to 20x chart above
Two Figures	5, 6, 14, 15	10 to 20x chart above

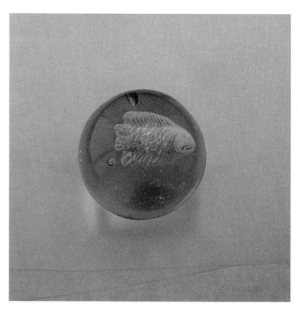

I-4-2. Fish, 1 7/8". *Courtesy of Wayne Sanders.*

I-4-3. Fish, 1 1/2". *Courtesy of Trudy Christian.*

I-4-4. Fish, dolphin, 1". *Courtesy of Stan Block.*

I-4-1. Fish, 1 5/8". *Courtesy of Stan Block.*

I-4-5. Fish, two fish, 1 1/2". *Courtesy of Stan Block.*

I-4-6. Fish, two fish, 1 1/2". *Courtesy of Jerry Biern.*

I-4-7. Frog, 1 3/4". *Courtesy of Jerry Biern.*

I-4-8. Frog, 1 3/8". *Courtesy of Jerry Biern.*

I-4-9. Frog, 1 7/8". *Courtesy of Stan Block.*

I-4-10. Frog, 1 5/8". *Courtesy of Stan Block.*

I-4-11. Iguana, 1 1/2". *Courtesy of Jerry Biern.*

I-4-12. Lizard, 1 1/4". *Courtesy of Jerry Biern.*

78

I-4-13. Lizard, 1 1/2". *Courtesy of Wilburn Powell.*

I-4-14. Lizard/worm, lizard on one side, 1 5/8". *Courtesy of Wayne Sanders.*

I-4-15. Lizard/worm, worm on reverse, reverse of I-4-14, 1 5/8". *Courtesy of Wayne Sanders.*

I-4-16. Lobster, on a plate, 1 3/4". *Courtesy of Jerry Biern.*

I-4-17. Lobster, on a plate, 1 3/4". *Courtesy of Jerry Biern.*

I-4-18. Lobster, 1 7/8". *Courtesy of Stan Block.*

I-4-19. Newt, 1 1/2". *Courtesy of Stan Block.*

I-4-20. Otter, 2 1/8". *Courtesy of Stan Block.*

I-4-21. Otter, 1 5/8". *Courtesy of Stan Block.*

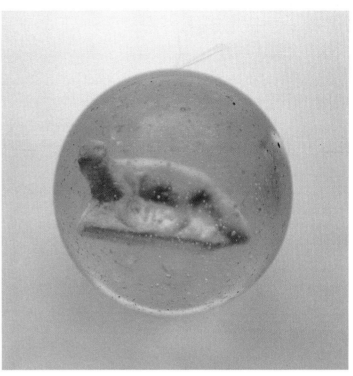

I-4-22. Seal, 1 1/2". *Courtesy of Stan Block.*

I-4-23. Snail, 1 3/4". *Courtesy of Bernie Benavidez.*

I-4-24. Turtle, 1 1/4". *Courtesy of Jeff Yale.*

I-4-25. Turtle, 1 1/4". *Courtesy of Jerry Biern.*

I-4-26. Turtle, purple back, 1 3/8". *Courtesy of Stan Block.*

I-4-27. Whale, 2 1/16". *Courtesy of Bill Sweet.*

I-4-28. Fish, has a ghost core and a piece of another figure, 1 5/8". *Courtesy of Dave Terrell.*

I-4-29. Sea lion, 1 3/4". *Courtesy of Lloyd Huffer.*

I-4-30. Sea lion, rear view of I-4-29, 1 3/4". *Courtesy of Lloyd Huffer.*

I-4-31. Beaver, 1 3/4". *Courtesy of Jeff Yale.*

I-4-32. Beaver, green glass, 1 3/4". *Courtesy of Wilburn Powell.*

I-4-33. Beaver, 1 1/2". *Courtesy of Block's Box.*

Birds and Fowl

Bat	Eagle	Harps Eagle	Pheasant	Swan
Bird	Emu	Hen	Pigeon	Turkey
Chick	Falcon	Love Birds	Quail	Vulture
Crane	Goose	Owl	Rooster	
Duck	Grouse	Parrot	Seagull	

Size	Mint	Near Mint	Good	Collectible
under 1"	$200.-	$150.-	$50.-	$30.-
1" to 1 3/16"	$150.-	$100.-	$50.-	$30.-
1 1/4" to 2"	$175.-	$100.-	$50.-	$30.-
over 2"	$250.-	$150.-	$50.-	$30.-

Premiums For:

Unusual figures or special features such as donut holes or secondary items	1x to 10x
Unusual poses	1x to 5x
Multiple figures	3x to 25x
Painted figures or colored glass (but not light tints)	5x to 25x

Deductions For:

Buffed surface	10% to 20%
Off center (depending on degree)	20% to 40%
Ground and polished surface	20%
Annealing fractures or missing parts	20% to 50%
Trapped air bubbles that obscure view	20% to 40%

Examples

	Photo #'s	
Unusual Figures	9, 20 thru 23, 25, 28, 33, 34, 35, 82	3 to 10x chart above
Colored Figure	39	10x chart above
Colored glass	5, 20, 69, 79	10 to 20x chart above
Two Figures	42 thru 47	5 to 15x chart above

I-5-2. Bat, 1 7/8". *Courtesy of Jerry Biern.*

I-5-3. Bat, reverse of I-5-2, 1 7/8". *Courtesy of Jerry Biern.*

I-5-1. Bat, 1 3/8". *Courtesy of Hansel de Sousa.*

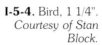**I-5-4.** Bird, 1 1/4". *Courtesy of Stan Block.*

I-5-5. Bird, green glass, 1 3/8". *Courtesy of Wilburn Powell.*

I-5-6. Bird, 2". *Courtesy of anonymous.*

I-5-7. Bird, 1 1/2". *Courtesy of Jerry Biern.*

I-5-8. Chick, 1 1/2". *Courtesy of Jeff Yale.*

I-5-9. Crane, eating a fish, 1 7/8". *Courtesy of Stan Block.*

I-5-10. Crane, 1 3/8". *Courtesy of anonymous.*

I-5-11. Duck, 1 1/2". *Courtesy of Stan Block.*

I-5-12. Duck, 1 1/2". *Courtesy of Marble Collectors' Society.*

I-5-13. Duck, 1 3/8". *Courtesy of Stan Block.*

I-5-14. Duck, 1 1/2". *Courtesy of Jerry Biern.*

I-5-15. Duck, 1 1/2". *Courtesy of Jeff Yale.*

I-5-16. Eagle, 1 1/8". *Courtesy of Stan Block.*

I-5-17. Eagle, 1 5/8". *Courtesy of Stan Block.*

I-5-18. Eagle, 1 3/4". *Courtesy of anonymous.*

I-5-19. Eagle, 2 1/4". *Courtesy of anonymous.*

I-5-20. Eagle, teal blue glass, 1 7/8". *Courtesy of Block's Box.*

I-5-21. Eagle, Federal Eagle holding cannons, 2 1/16". *Courtesy of Jerry Biern.*

I-5-22. Eagle, Federal Eagle with shield and branches, 1 1/2". *Courtesy of Elliot Pincus.*

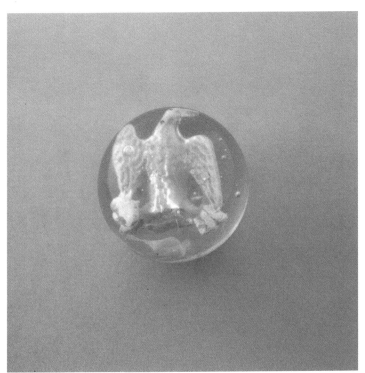

I-5-23. Eagle, reverse of I-5-22, 1 1/2". *Courtesy of Elliot Pincus.*

I-5-24. Eagle, 7/8". *Courtesy of Carrol Collier.*

I-5-25. Eagle, Federal Eagle holding arrows, 1 1/2". *Courtesy of Wilburn Powell.*

I-5-26. Eagle, totem pole type, 1 7/8". *Courtesy of Jerry Biern.*

I-5-27. Eagle, totem pole type, 1 3/4". *Courtesy of Stan Block.*

I-5-28. Emu, 1 3/8". *Courtesy of Dale Mendenhall.*

I-5-29. Falcon, 1 3/4". *Courtesy of Block's Box.*

I-5-30. Goose, 1 3/8". *Courtesy of Stan Block.*

I-5-31. Goose, 1 3/4". *Courtesy of Jeff Yale.*

I-5-32. Goose, different view of I-5-31, 1 3/4". *Courtesy of Jeff Yale.*

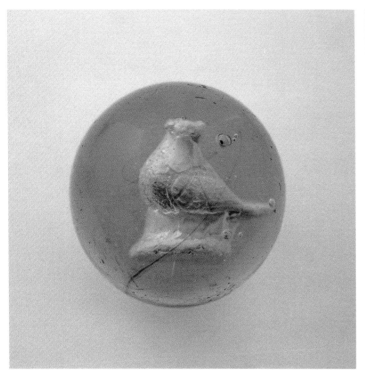

I-5-33. Grouse, 1 7/8". *Courtesy of Stan Block.*

I-5-34. Grouse, ruffled grouse, 1 1/2". *Courtesy of Stan Block.*

I-5-35. Harps eagle, 2 5/8". *Courtesy of Bernie Benavidez.*

I-5-36. Hen, 2". *Courtesy of Elliot Pincus.*

I-5-37. Hen, 1 1/2". *Courtesy of anonymous.*

I-5-38. Hen, 1 3/8". *Courtesy of Jeff Yale.*

I-5-39. Hen, blue tail & chest, brown wings & crown, green base, black eyes & beak, 1 3/8". *Courtesy of Wilburn Powell.*

I-5-40. Hen, 1 1/2". *Courtesy of Wilburn Powell.*

I-5-41. Hen, 1 1/2". *Courtesy of Stan Block.*

I-5-42. Hen and Rooster, 2". *Courtesy of Pat Jamieson & South Jersey Marble Club.*

I-5-43. Love birds, 2". *Courtesy of Stan Block.*

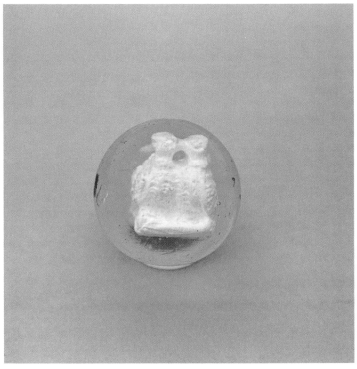

I-5-44. Love birds, 1 1/8" . *Courtesy of Jeff Yale.*

Yale.

I-5-46. Love birds, wings half open, 1 1/2". *Courtesy of Stan Block.*

I-5-47 . Love birds, reverse of I-5-46, 1 1/2". *Courtesy of Stan Block.*

I-5-48. Owl, 1 1/2". *Courtesy of Les Jones.*

I-5-49. Owl, 1 5/8". *Courtesy of Stan Block.*

I-5-50. Owl, 1 7/8". *Courtesy of Stan Block.*

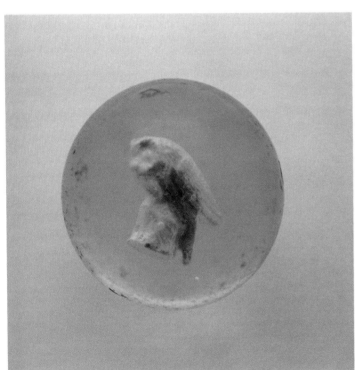

I-5-51. Owl, 1 5/8". *Courtesy of anonymous.*

I-5-52. Owl, 15/16". *Courtesy of anonymous.*

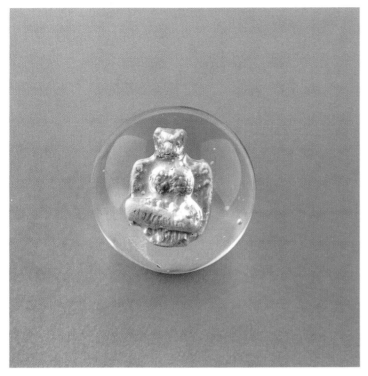

I-5-53. Owl, 1 1/8". *Courtesy of Stan Block.*

I-5-54. Owl, 1 7/8". *Courtesy of Stan Block.*

I-5-55. Owl, 1 5/8". *Courtesy of Jerry Biern.*

I-5-56. Owl, 1 3/8". *Courtesy of Stan Block.*

I-5-57. Owl, 2". *Courtesy of Jerry Biern.*

I-5-58. Owl, reverse of I-5-57, 2". *Courtesy of Jerry Biern.*

I-5-59. Owl, 2 1/8". *Courtesy of Stan Block.*

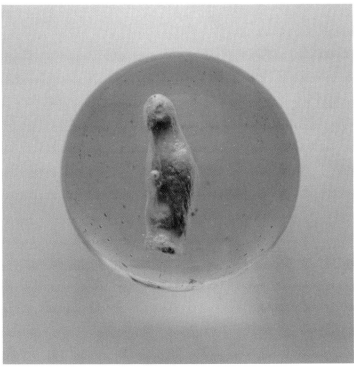

I-5-60. Parrot, 1 3/4". *Courtesy of Stan Block.*

I-5-61. Parrot, 1 7/8". *Courtesy of Block's Box.*

I-5-62. Parrot, 1 1/2". *Courtesy of Stan Block.*

I-5-63. Parrot, 1 7/8". *Courtesy of anonymous.*

I-5-64. Pheasant, 1 5/8". *Courtesy of Jerry Biern.*

I-5-65. Pheasant, 1 7/8". *Courtesy of Jerry Biern.*

I-5-66. Pigeon, 1 1/4". *Courtesy of Stan Block.*

I-5-67. Pigeon, 1 1/2". *Courtesy of Stan Block.*

I-5-68. Pigeon, donut hole type, 2 1/8". *Courtesy of Jerry Biern.*

I-5-69. Pigeon, amethyst glass, 1 1/2". *Courtesy of Stan Block.*

I-5-70. Pigeon, 1 1/2". *Courtesy of anonymous.*

I-5-71. Pigeon, 1 1/8". *Courtesy of anonymous.*

I-5-72. Quail, 1 3/4". *Courtesy of Stan Block.*

I-5-73. Quail, 1 7/8". *Courtesy of Scott Strasburger.*

I-5-74. Rooster, 1 3/4". *Courtesy of Stan Block.*

I-5-75. Rooster, 2 3/8". *Courtesy of Bill Sweet.*

I-5-76. Rooster, 2". *Courtesy of Stan Block.*

I-5-77. Rooster, 1 1/8". *Courtesy of Stan Block.*

I-5-78. Rooster, 1 3/8". *Courtesy of anonymous.*

I-5-79. Rooster, yellow glass, 1 1/4". *Courtesy of Jeff Yale.*

I-5-80. Rooster, 1 1/4". *Courtesy of Stan Block.*

I-5-81. Rooster, reverse of I-5-80, 1 1/4". *Courtesy of Stan Block.*

I-5-82. Seagull, 1 1/8". *Courtesy of Stan Block.*

I-5-83. Swan, 1 1/4". *Courtesy of Stan Block.*

I-5-84. Swan, 1 1/4". *Courtesy of Jerry Biern.*

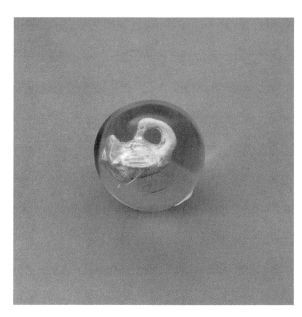
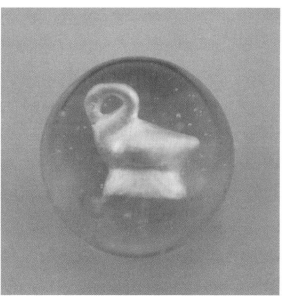

I-5-85. Swan, donut hole, 1 3/8". *Courtesy of Jeff Yale.*

I-5-86. Swan, donut hole, 1 3/8". *Courtesy of Block's Box.*

I-5-87. Turkey, 1 3/8". *Courtesy of Les Jones.*

I-5-88. Turkey, 1 3/8". *Courtesy of Wilburn Powell.*

I-5-89. Turkey, 1 1/2". *Courtesy of Stan Block.*

I-5-90. Vulture, 1 3/4". *Courtesy of Wayne Sanders.*

Section II: Human Figures

Barrister	Mandolin Player
Beethoven	Old Man
Boy	Papoose
Bride	Peasant
Cherub	Peasant Dancers
Child	President Garfield &
Clown	Chester Arthur
Columbus	Prospector
Court Jester	Teddy Roosevelt
Custer	Soldier
Dutch Boy	George Washington
Girl	Kaiser Wilhelm
Franz Josef	Witch
Jenny Lind	Woman

Size	Mint	Near Mint	Good	Collectible
under 1"	$400.-	$300.-	$150.-	$75.-
1" to 1 3/16"	$400.-	$300.-	$150.-	$75.-
1 1/4" to 2"	$400.-	$300.-	$150.-	$75.-
over 2"	$500.-	$400.-	$150.-	$75.-

Premiums For:

Unusual figures or special features such as donut holes or secondary items	1x to 10x
Unusual poses	1x to 5x
Multiple figures	3x to 25x
Painted figures or colored glass (but not light tints)	5x to 25x

Deductions For:

Buffed surface	10% to 20%
Off center (depending on degree)	20% to 40%
Ground and polished surface	20%
Annealing fractures or missing parts	20% to 50%
Trapped air bubbles that obscure view	20% to 40%

Examples

	Photo #'s	
Unusual Figures or poses	25, 27, 28, 32, 37 thru 42A, 43, 47, 52, 53, 54, 59, 60, 63 thru 81	3 to 10x chart above
Colored Figures	50, 51, 55, 56, 84 thru 88	5 to 10x chart above
Colored glass	36, 42B	8 to 15x chart above
Double Figures	57, 58, 61, 62	5 to 15x chart above

II-1. Naked boy, 1 3/8". *Courtesy of Wayne Sanders.*

II-2. Naked boy, 1 3/4". *Courtesy of Jerry Biern.*

II-3. Naked boy, 2". *Courtesy of Block's Box.*

II-4. Naked boy, reverse of II-3, 2". *Courtesy of Block's Box.*

II-5. Girl praying, 1 1/2". *Courtesy of Stan Block.*

II-6. Girl praying, 1 1/2". *Courtesy of Wilburn Powell.*

107

II-7. Girl with mallet and ball, 1 3/4". *Courtesy of Block's Box.*

II-8. Girl with mallet and ball, 1 1/2". *Courtesy of Jeff Yale.*

II-9. Child with book, 2". *Courtesy of Block's Box.*

II-10. Child with book, 2". *Courtesy of Stan Block.*

II-11. Girl with book, 2". *Courtesy of Block's Box.*

II-12. Girl crawling, 2". *Courtesy of Stan Block.*

II-13. Girl crawling, paperweight and marble - paperweight is 2 1/8" d. Marble is 1 3/4". *Courtesy of Stan Block.*

II-14. Girl in chair, chair is upside down, 1 3/4". *Courtesy of Block's Box.*

II-15. Girl holding a doll, 1 7/8". *Courtesy of Stan Block.*

II-16. Seated peasant, 1 1/4". *Courtesy of Jerry Biern.*

II-17. Seated peasant, side view of II-16, 1 1/4". *Courtesy of Jerry Biern.*

II-18. Seated peasant, 1 3/8". *Courtesy of Stan Block.*

II-19. Little Boy Blue, 1 7/8". *Courtesy of Block's Box.*

II-20. Boy in uniform, 1 1/4". *Courtesy of Wayne Sanders.*

II-21. Colonial boy in a chair, 1 3/8". *Courtesy of Jeff Yale.*

II-22. Old man on a potty, 1 5/8". *Courtesy of Wayne Sanders.*

II-23. Old man on a potty, 1 3/8". *Courtesy of Jeff Yale.*

II-24. Old man on a potty, reverse of II-23, 1 3/8". *Courtesy of Jeff Yale.*

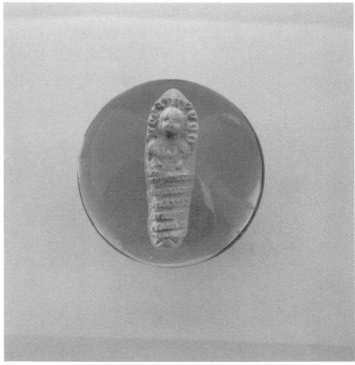

II-25. Drummer boy, 1 1/8". *Courtesy of Bernie Benavidez.*

II-26. Papoose, 2 1/8". *Courtesy of Block's Box.*

II-27. Bride, 1 3/8". *Courtesy of Jeff Yale.*

II-28. Bride, reverse of II-27, 1 3/8". *Courtesy of Jeff Yale.*

II-29. Kate Greenway, 1 3/4". *Courtesy of Jeff Yale.*

II-30. Kate Greenway, 1 1/2". *Courtesy of Stan Block.*

II-31. Standing woman, 1 7/8". *Courtesy of Les Jones.*

II-32. Girl on a wall, 1 1/2". *Courtesy of Block's Box.*

II-33. Lady with a basket, 1 3/8". *Courtesy of Jeff Yale.*

II-34. Lady with dog & basket , 1 7/8". *Courtesy of Stan Block.*

II-35. Lady with dog & basket, 1 7/8". *Courtesy of Jeff Yale.*

II-36. Lady with basket, green glass, 1 1/4". *Courtesy of Wilburn Powell.*

II-37. Wicked witch, 1 3/8". *Courtesy of Hansel de Sousa.*

II-38. Wicked witch, 1 1/2". *Courtesy of Joyce Johnston.*

II-39. George Washington, 1 3/8". *Courtesy of Jerry Biern.*

II-39a. George Washington, 1 5/8". *Courtesy of Elliot Pincus.*

II-40. Barrister, 1 1/2". *Courtesy of Jerry Biern.*

II-41. Revolutionary soldier, 1 9/16". *Courtesy of Jeff Yale.*

116

II-42. Mandolin player, 1 3/4". *Courtesy of Jeff Yale.*

II-42a. Mandolin player, 1 5/8". *Courtesy of Elliot Pincus.*

II-42b. Mandolin player, green glass, 1 3/8". *Courtesy of Wilburn Powell.*

II-43. Prospector, 1 3/4". *Courtesy of Jerry Biern.*

117

II-44. Court jester, 1 1/4". *Courtesy of Jeff Yale.*

II-45. Court jester, 1 1/2". *Courtesy of Block's Box.*

II-46. Court jester, 1 3/8". *Courtesy of Jerry Biern.*

II-47. Dutch boy, 1 3/8". *Courtesy of Jeff Yale.*

II-48. Clown, 1 5/8". *Courtesy of Stan Block.*

II-49. Clown, 1 5/8". *Courtesy of Stan Block.*

II-50. Clown, painted hat and shoes, 2". *Courtesy of Jerry Biern.*

II-51. Clown, painted hat and shoes, 1 7/8". *Courtesy of Jeff Yale.*

119

II-52. Colonial man on a horse, also known as George Washington, 1 7/8". *Courtesy of Stan Block.*

II-53. Man on a horse with a donut hole, 1 5/8". *Courtesy of Hansel de Sousa.*

II-54. Man on a horse with a donut hole, 1 5/8". *Courtesy of Jerry Biern.*

II-55. Seated woman, amber glass, 2". *Courtesy of Wilburn Powell.*

II-56. Seated girl, brown hair, 1 1/2". *Courtesy of Elliot Pincus.*

II-57. Peasant dancers, 2 3/8". *Courtesy of Stan Block.*

II-58. Peasant dancers, reverse of II-57, 2 3/8". *Courtesy of Stan Block.*

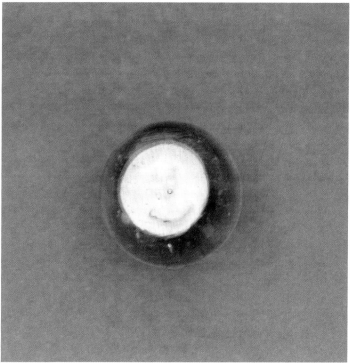

II-59. Face on a disc, 1 3/8". *Courtesy of Elloit Pincus.*

121

II-60. Face on a disc, reverse of II-59, 1 3/8". *Courtesy of Elliot Pincus.*

II-61. Seated boy & girl, 1 3/8". *Courtesy of Stan Block.*

II-62. Seated boy & girl, reverse of II-61, 1 3/8". *Courtesy of Stan Block.*

II-63. Cherub in a blanket, 2 1/16". *Courtesy of Jerry Biern.*

II-65. Cherub in a blanket, 2 1/16".
Courtesy of Wilburn Powell.

II-64. Cherub in a blanket, reverse of II-63, 2 1/16". *Courtesy of Jerry Biern.*

II-66. T. Roosevelt, 1 1/2". *Courtesy of Bert Cohen.*

II-67. Columbus, 1 3/8". *Courtesy of Jerry Biern.*

II-68. Columbus, slight variation from II-67, 1 7/8". *Courtesy of Jerry Biern.*

II-69. Franz Josef, 1 1/2". *Courtesy of Jerry Biern.*

II-70. Franz Josef, 1 3/4". *Courtesy of Wayne Sanders.*

II-71. Franz Josef, different view of II-70, 1 3/4". *Courtesy of Wayne Sanders.*

II-72. Kaiser Wilhelm, on a disc, one side only, 2". *Courtesy of Block's Box.*

II-73. Kaiser Wilhelm, 1 3/4". *Courtesy of Jeff Yale.*

II-74. Kaiser Wilhelm, reverse of II-73, 1 3/4". *Courtesy of Jeff Yale.*

II-75. President Garfield on a wreathed heart, 1 5/8". *Courtesy of Block's Box.*

II-76. V. P. Chester Arthur, reverse of II-75, 1 5/8". *Courtesy of Block's Box.*

II-77. Beethoven, 1 7/8". *Courtesy of Block's Box.*

II-78. Beethoven, different view, 1 7/8". *Courtesy of Block's Box.*

II-79. Two sided bust of General George Custer, 1 3/4". *Courtesy of Jerry Biern.*

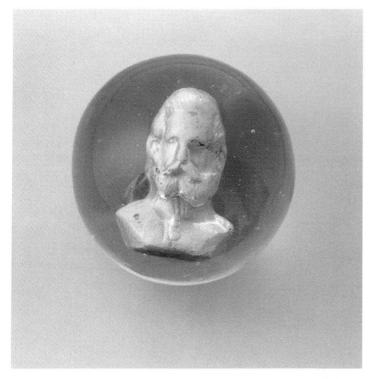

II-80. Two sided bust of General George Custer, one side, 1 3/4". *Courtesy of Jerry Biern.*

II-81. General George Custer , second side, 1 3/4". *Courtesy of Jerry Biern.*

II-82. Jenny Lind, 1 1/16". *Courtesy of Gary Huxford.*

II-83. Jenny Lind, 1 3/4". *Courtesy of Block's Box.*

127

II-84. Jenny Lind, painted figure, 1 1/8". *Courtesy of Jerry Biern.*

II-85. Jenny Lind, painted figure - before restoration, 1 1/2". *Courtesy of Stan Block.*

II-86. Jenny Lind, side view of II-85, 1 1/2". *Courtesy of Stan Block.*

II-87. Jenny Lind, painted figure - after restoration, 1 1/2". *Courtesy of Stan Block.*

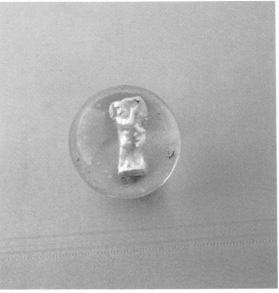

II-88. Jenny Lind, painted figure - after restoration - reverse of II-87, 1 1/2". *Courtesy of Stan Block.*

II-89 . Boy carrying a basket, 1 1/8". *Courtesy of Elliot Pincus.*

Section III: Religious and Mythical Characters

Airewolf Demon   Gnome   Moses in   Punch & Judy
Angel   Dog or   Leprechaun a Basket   Rabbit in Suit
Ape Man   Ape Man   Mermaid   Pan   Santa Claus
Crucifix Gargoyle   Monkey Man Phoenix   Squirrel in Suit

Size	Mint	Near Mint	Good	Collectible
under 1"	$400.-	$300.-	$150.-	$75.-
1" to 1 3/16"	$400.-	$300.-	$150.-	$75.-
1 1/4" to 2"	$400.-	$300.-	$150.-	$75.-
over 2"	$500.-	$400.-	$150.-	$75.-

Premiums For:

Unusual figures or special features such as donut holes or secondary items	1x to 10x
Unusual poses	1x to 5x
Multiple figures	3x to 25x
Painted figures or colored glass (but not light tints)	5x to 25x

Deductions For:

Buffed surface	10% to 20%
Off center (depending on degree)	20% to 40%
Ground and polished surface	20%
Annealing fractures or missing parts	20% to 50%
Trapped air bubbles that obscure view	20% to 40%

Examples	Photo #'s	
Unusual Figures or Poses	10, 16, 26 thru 28, 33 thru 38, 49 thru 55	3 to 10x chart above
Colored Figures	7, 8, 9, 14, 15, 48	5 to 10x chart above
Colored Glass	19, 31, 32, 56	8 to 15x chart above
Double Figures	57 thru 59	5 to 10x chart above

III-1. Angel, 1 5/8". *Courtesy of Stan Block.*

III-2. Angel, 1 1/2". *Courtesy of anonymous.*

III-3. Angel, 1 5/8. *Courtesy of Jeff Yale.*

III-4. Angel, 1 3/4". *Courtesy of Stan Block.*

III-5. Angel, 2 3/8". *Courtesy of Stan Block.*

III-6. Angel, 1 5/8". *Courtesy of anonymous.*

III-7. Angel, colored figure, 1 3/8". *Courtesy of Stan Block.*

III-8. Angel, reverse of III-7, 1 3/8". *Courtesy of Stan Block.*

III-9. Angel, colored figure, 1 5/8". *Courtesy of Hansel de Sousa.*

III-10. Angel, cherub, 1 3/4". *Courtesy of Block's Box.*

III-11. Angel, 1 3/4". *Courtesy of Stan Block.*

III-12. Angel, 1 3/8". *Courtesy of Jerry Biern.*

III-13. Angel, reverse of III-12, 1 3/8". *Courtesy of Jerry Biern.*

III-14. Angel, colored figure, 1 1/2". *Courtesy of Stan Block.*

III-15. Angel, reverse of III-14, 1 1/2". *Courtesy of Stan Block.*

132

III-16. Angel, cherub, 1 1/16". *Courtesy of Jerry Biern.*

III-17. Moses in a basket, 1 1/2". *Courtesy of Jerry Biern.*

III-18. Moses in a basket, 1 3/8". *Courtesy of Jerry Biern.*

III-19. Moses in a basket, blue glass, 1 1/16". *Courtesy of Jerry Biern.*

III-20. Crucifix, 1 3/4". *Courtesy of Stan Block.*

III-21. Crucifix, 1 1/2". *Courtesy of Stan Block.*

III-22. Crucifix, 2". *Courtesy of Wilburn Powell.*

III-23. Crucifix, 2". *Courtesy of Marble Collectors' Society.*

III-24. Crucifix, 2 1/4". *Courtesy of Jeff Yale.*

III-25. Crucifix, 1 3/4". *Courtesy of Jeff Yale.*

III-26. Santa Claus, 1 1/2". *Courtesy of Jerry Biern.*

III-27. Santa Claus, side view of III-26, 1 1/2". *Courtesy of Jerry Biern.*

III-34. Mermaid, side view of III-33, 1 1/2". *Courtesy of Jeff Yale.*

III-35. Demon, 1 3/4". *Courtesy of Jerry Biern.*

III-36. Ape Man, in uniform, holding a hat, 1 3/4". *Courtesy of Block's Box.*

III-37. Ape Man, side view of III-36, 1 3/4". *Courtesy of Block's Box.*

III-38. Ape Man, in colonial garb, 1 5/8". *Courtesy of Stan Block.*

III-39. Monkey Man, organ grinder monkey or monkey man eating an apple and wearing a hat and coat, 1 1/8". *Courtesy of Block's Box.*

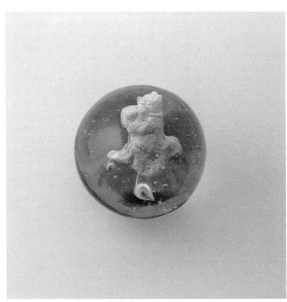

III-40. Rabbit, in a suit, reading a book, 1 5/8". *Courtesy of Jerry Biern.*

III-41. Squirrel, wearing a suit, 1 3/8". *Courtesy of Jerry Biern.*

III-42. Dog or Ape, wearing a hat or shawl, 1 1/2". *Courtesy of Stan Block.*

III-43. Dog or Ape, wearing a hat or shawl, 1 3/8". *Courtesy of Jerry Biern.*

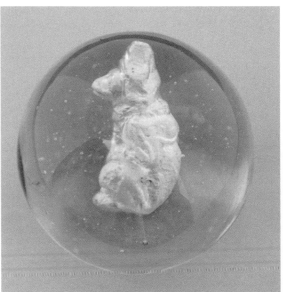

III-44. Monkey Man, wearing a hat, 2". *Courtesy of Block's Box.*

III-45. Monkey Man, side view of III-44, 2". *Courtesy of Block's Box.*

III-46. Dog or Bear, wearing a hat, 1 5/8". *Courtesy of Stan Block.*

III-47. Dog, wearing a hat and long coat, 1 3/8". *Courtesy of Stan Block.*

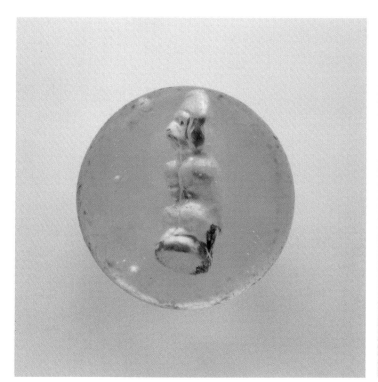

III-48. Dog, wearing a hat - colored figure, 1 5/8". *Courtesy of Stan Block.*

III-49. Aire-wolf, 1 5/8". *Courtesy of Stan Block.*

III-50. Phoenix bird, 1 3/4". *Courtesy of Jeff Yale.*

III-51. Gargoyle, 1 1/4". *Courtesy of Stan Block.*

III-52. Gargoyle, 2 1/8". *Courtesy of Stan Block.*

III-53. Gargoyle, 2 1/8". *Courtesy of Bernie Benavidez.*

III-54. Gnome on a potty, 1 3/4". *Courtesy of Elliot Pincus.*

III-55. Gnome on a potty, reverse of III-54, 1 3/4". *Courtesy of Elliot Pincus.*

III-56. Leprechaun, with coat, hat, and gun in blue glass, 1 1/8". *Courtesy of Wilburn Powell.*

III-57. Punch & Judy, 1 3/4". *Courtesy of Bernie Benavidez.*

III-58. Punch & Judy, reverse of III-57, 1 3/4". *Courtesy of Bernie Benavidez.*

III-59. Punch & Judy, side view of III-57 and III-58, 1 3/4". *Courtesy of Bernie Benavidez.*

Section IV: Inanimate Subjects

Size	Half Dime Indian Head Penny Numbers		Numbers on a Coin Disc Pocket Watch	
	Mint	Near Mint	Good	Collectible
under 1"	$400.-	$300.-	$100.-	$75.-
1" to 1 3/16"	$400.-	$300.-	$100.-	$75.-
1 1/4" to 2"	$400.-	$300.-	$100.-	$75.-
over 2"	$500.-	$400.-	$100.-	$75.-

Premiums For:

Unusual figures or special features such as donut holes or secondary items	1x to 10x
Unusual poses	1x to 5x
Multiple figures	3x to 25x
Painted figures or colored glass (but not light tints)	5x to 25x

Deductions For:

Buffed surface	10% to 20%
Off center (depending on degree)	20% to 40%
Ground and polished surface	20%
Annealing fractures or missing parts	20% to 50%
Trapped air bubbles that obscure view	20% to 40%

Examples	Photo #'s	
Unusual Figures or Poses	32 thru 35, 38	2 to 8x chart above
Colored Figures	2, 4, 6, 9, 11, 36, 37	5 to 8x chart above
Colored Glass	21 thru 23	5 to 8x chart above

IV-2. #1, green figure, 1 5/8". *Courtesy of Wilburn Powell.*

IV-3. #2, 1 5/8". *Courtesy of Stan Block.*

IV-1. #1, 1 1/2". *Courtesy of Stan Block.*

IV-4. #2, blue figure, 1 5/8". *Courtesy of anonymous.*

IV-5. #3, 1 3/8". *Courtesy of Stan Block.*

IV-6. #3, blue figure, 1 1/2". *Courtesy of Block's Box.*

IV-7. #4, 1 5/8". *Courtesy of Stan Block.*

IV-8. #5, 1 5/8". *Courtesy of Stan Block.*

IV-9. #5, green figure, 1 5/8". *Courtesy of Wayne Sanders.*

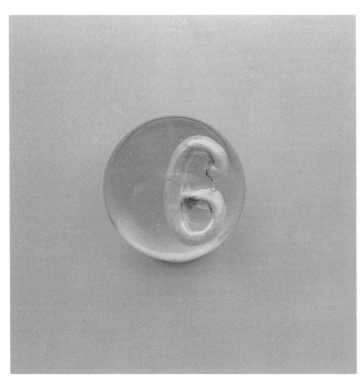

IV-10. #6, 1 3/8". *Courtesy of Stan Block.*

IV-11. #6, green figure, 1 5/8". *Courtesy of Marble Collectors' Society.*

IV-12. #7, 1 5/8". *Courtesy of Stan Block.*

IV-13. #8, 1 5/8". *Courtesy of Stan Block.*

IV-14. #9, 1 1/2". *Courtesy of Stan Block.*

IV-15. #0 on a coin, 1 1/2". *Courtesy of Block's Box.*

IV-16. #1 on a coin, No Photo.

IV-17. #2 on a coin, 1 3/4". *Courtesy of Block's Box.*

IV-18. #2 on a coin, reverse of IV-17. *Courtesy of Block's Box.*

IV-19. #3 on a coin, 1 5/8". *Courtesy of Block's Box.*

IV-20. #4 on a coin, 1 5/8". *Courtesy of Block's Box.*

IV-21. #4 on a coin, amethyst glass, 1 3/8". *Courtesy of Jeff Yale.*

146

IV-22. #5 on a coin, amethyst glass, 1 1/2". *Courtesy of Block's Box.*

IV-23. #5 on a coin, amethyst glass - reverse of IV-22, 1 1/2". *Courtesy of Block's Box.*

IV-24. #6 on a coin, 1 3/8". *Courtesy of Jeff Yale.*

IV-25. #6 on a coin, 1 3/4". *Courtesy of Block's Box.*

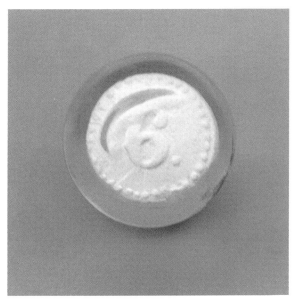 

IV-26. #7 on a coin, 1 1/2". *Courtesy of Block's Box.*

IV-27. #7 on a coin, reverse of IV-26, 1 1/2". *Courtesy of Block's Box.*

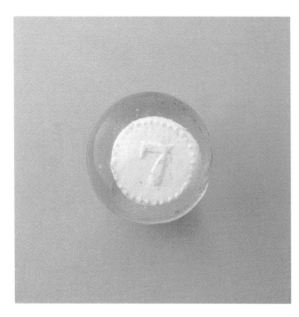

IV-28. #7 on a coin, 1 1/2". *Courtesy of Elliot Pincus.*

IV-29. #8 on a coin, 1 3/4". *Courtesy of Block's Box.*

IV-30. #9 on a coin, 1 1/4". *Courtesy of Jeff Yale.*

IV-31. #10 on a coin, 1 3/4". *Courtesy of Block's Box.*

IV-32. Pocket watch, 1 3/4". *Courtesy of Stan Block.*

IV-33. Pocket watch, reverse of IV-32, 1 3/4". *Courtesy of Stan Block.*

IV-34. Half dime, 1 1/4". *Courtesy of Jerry Biern.*

IV-35. Half dime, reverse of IV-34, 1 1/4". *Courtesy of Jerry Biern.*

IV-36. Unusual #1, blue on a white base, 1 3/8". *Courtesy of Wilburn Powell.*

IV-37. Unusual #1, reverse of IV-36, 1 3/8". *Courtesy of Wilburn Powell.*

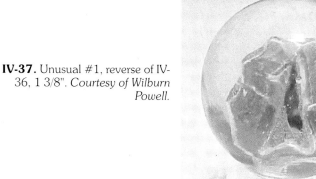

IV-38. Penny, Indian Head, 1 5/8". *Courtesy of Elliot Pincus.*

149

Section V: Other

Miscellaneous

V-1-5. Unknown, 1". *Courtesy of Stan Block.*

V-1-6. Unknown, reverse of V-1-5, 1". *Courtesy of Stan Block.*

V-1-7. Unknown, 1 5/8". *Courtesy of Stan Block.*

V-1-8. Unknown, reverse of V-1-7, 1 5/8". *Courtesy of Stan Block.*

Opposite page, left to right:
V-1-1. Two sided, stag's head, 1 3/4". *Courtesy of Block's Box.*

V-1-2. Two sided, reverse of V-1-1, goat standing over boy, 1 3/4". *Courtesy of Block's Box.*

V-1-3. Two sided, stag's head, 2". *Courtesy of Stan Block.*

V-1-4. Two sided, stag's head, reverse V-1-3, 2". *Courtesy of Stan Block.*

V-1-9. Ghost core, appears as a cow, 1 1/4". *Courtesy of Marble Collectors' Society.*

V-1-10. Miscellaneous, large board with 3/4" to 1" sulphides; in blue glass are a girl & boy, 3/4" to 1". *Courtesy of Wilburn Powell.*

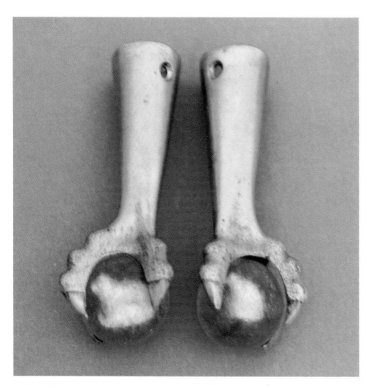

V-1-11. Stool legs, pair of claw feet, 1 1/2". *Courtesy of Trudy Christian.*

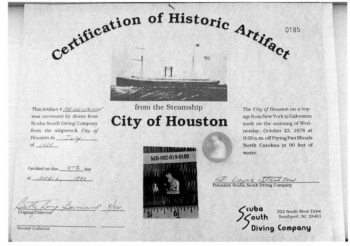

V-1-12. From shipwreck, includes certificate, 1 3/8". *Courtesy of Marble Collectors' Society.*

V-1-13. Box of sulphides. *Courtesy of Hansel DeSousa.*

V-1-14. Sulphide pattern, mold for sulphide - probably for a paperweight, 3" square. *Courtesy of Stan Block.*

V-1-15. Three figure sulphide: fish, dog, and duck. *Courtesy of Dave Terrell.*

V-1-16. Three figure sulphide, second view of V-1-15. *Courtesy of Dave Terrell.*

V-1-17. Seated girl, sulphide, matching figure in a marble and a paperweight. *Courtesy of Stan Block.*

153

Italian Sulphides

In the late 1960s, a New York City importer commissioned an Italian firm to produce a number of sulphide marbles. These consisted of the figures #0 to #9, each in a separate marble. Also, three different animal figures were produced (horse, cow, and pig). Each of these were in a marble with a carpet of colored glass flecks directly beneath the figure. None of these items was signed. How- ever, they can be identified because the sulphide figures have no silvery sheen and the glass of the marble is crystal clear. These were not very successful commercially, and relatively few were sold, and then only for a short period of time. They occasionally come up for private sale or auction.

V-2-1. #1, one side molded, other ground flat, 2 1/4". *Courtesy of Marble Collectors' Society.*

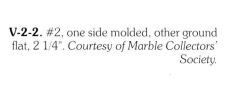

V-2-2. #2, one side molded, other ground flat, 2 1/4". *Courtesy of Marble Collectors' Society.*

V-2-3. #3, one side molded, other ground flat, 2 1/4". *Courtesy of Marble Collectors' Society.*

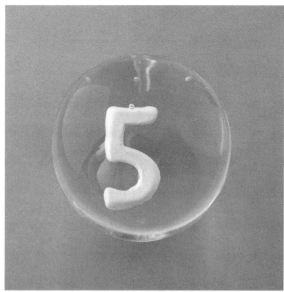

V-2-4. #4, one side molded, other ground flat, 2 1/4". *Courtesy of Marble Collectors' Society.*

V-2-5. #5, one side molded, other ground flat, 2 1/4". *Courtesy of Marble Collectors' Society.*

V-2-6. #6, one side molded, other ground flat, 2 1/4". *Courtesy of Marble Collectors' Society.*

V-2-7. #7, one side molded, other ground flat, 2 1/4". *Courtesy of Marble Collectors' Society.*

V-2-8. #8, one side molded, other ground flat, 2 1/4". *Courtesy of Marble Collectors' Society.*

V-2-9. #9, one side molded, other ground flat, 2 1/4". *Courtesy of Marble Collectors' Society.*

V-2-10. #0, one side molded, other ground flat, 2 1/4". *Courtesy of Marble Collectors' Society.*

V-2-11. Horse, one side molded, other ground flat, 2 1/8". *Courtesy of Marble Collectors' Society.*

V-2-12. Pig, one side molded, other ground flat, 2 1/8". *Courtesy of Marble Collectors' Society.*

V-2-13. Duck, one side molded, other ground flat, 2 1/8". *Courtesy of Marble Collectors' Society.*

California Sulphides

During 1993 and 1994 previously unknown Sulphides began to appear in the marketplace. The first, and largest group, was offered at marble shows on behalf of a California collector, hence, the term 'California Sulphides'.

A second, much smaller group, became available shortly thereafter through an antique dealer in Florida. A third group followed via a dealer in Nevada. The California group contained 85 marbles, the Florida group consisted of 19, and the Nevada offering was reported to contain 12 marbles. Many of the Florida and Nevada marbles contained the same figures as the California group.

Clear Glass - Single Figures (19)

Angel fish in a latticinio swirl
Bat in a latticino core swirl
Cat in a divided core swirl
Crucifix
(2) Exploded Sulphides
Hen in a single pontil cloud with mica
Horse
Man playing a mandolin
Metal Disc - #13
Metal Keyhole
Metal Lamp Knob
Number 6 in a divided core swirl
Number 07
Pirate in a divided core swirl
President Lincoln on a coin in a swirl
Sea Horse in a latticinio swirl
Sulphide swirl
Woman

Clear Glass - Double Figures (7)

Birds
Cats
Cat and Dog
(2) Dogs
Hens
Women

Clear Glass - Three Figures (2)

Birds
Cats

Amber Glass - Single Figures (44)

Angel's head with wings
Bat

(2) Bears
Bottle
(2) Buffalo/Bison
(2) Bulls
Cat
(2) Dogs
(3) Elephants
(2) Horses
(2) Lions
(3) Pigs
(2) Rabbits
(2) Rams
Rhinoceros
(3) Sea Horses
Skull
Vampire Bat
(11) Woman on a horse
(1) Woman on a horse with mica

Amber Glass - Double Figures (6)

Angel Fish
(2) Birds
(3) Fish

Other Colored Glass (5)

Bull in green glass
Two eagles in aqua glass
Mica in green glass
Mica in purple glass
President Jefferson on a coin in purple glass

Due to the types and the number of previously unknown figures, many collectors questioned the authenticity of these marbles. Over a period of two to three years, tests were run and research into the controversy continued. Since the original introduction, nothing conclusive has occurred, and collectors remain split as to whether these California Sulphides are originals, experimentals, or reproductions. To our knowledge, no additional marbles have appeared and the three groups have been assimilated into collections. Occasionally, when normal resales do occur in the market place, these marbles have sold in the range of $200 to $500 each.

Since there are so many pros and cons involved in this subject, and no definitive answers have come forward, we will limit this discourse in the hope there will be some new information in the future. Our purpose is to make the collecting public (new and old) aware of this group.

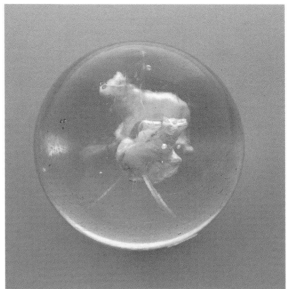

V-3-1. Lamb, cobalt blue glass, 1 3/8". *Courtesy of Jeff Yale.*

V-3-2. Two dogs, 2 1/8". *Courtesy of Jeff Yale.*

V-3-3. Rabbit, yellow tinted glass, 1 3/8". *Courtesy of Stan Block.*

V-3-4. Hippopotamus, 2 1/8". *Courtesy of Jeff Yale.*

V-3-5. Hippopotamus, with bird on back in cobalt blue glass, 2 1/8". *Courtesy of Stan Block.*

V-3-6. Lion, 2". *Courtesy of Bill Sweet.*

V-3-7. Pair of fish, 1 7/8". *Courtesy of anonymous.*

V-3-8. Sea Horse, dark amber glass, 1 3/8". *Courtesy of Jeff Yale.*

V-3-9. Pair of birds, yellow glass, 1 1/4". *Courtesy of Jeff Yale.*

V-3-10. Bird, 1 5/8". *Courtesy of anonymous.*

V-3-11. Bat, dark amber glass, 1 1/8". *Courtesy of Jeff Yale.*

V-3-12. Gargoyle, light yellow tint to glass, 1 3/8". *Courtesy of Stan Block.*

V-3-13. Two women with brown towels, 2 1/8". *Courtesy of Jeff Yale.*

V-3-14. Two women with brown towels, reverse view of V-3-13, 2 1/8". *Courtesy of Jeff Yale.*

V-3-16. Crucifix, 1 1/2". *Courtesy of Stan Block.*

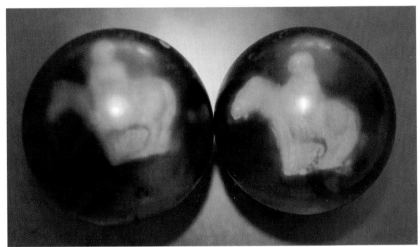

V-3-15. Women on horses, two marbles - women riding side saddle in amber glass, 1 5/8". *Courtesy of anonymous.*

V-3-17. #07, 1 7/8". *Courtesy of Larry Svacina.*

V-3-18. Sulphide in a swirl, 1 1/2". *Courtesy of Larry Svacina.*

160

Contemporary Sulphides

In order to fully cover sulphide marbles, we have included this discussion on contemporary handmade sulphide marbles. A number of contemporary glass artisans have crafted or are still creating sulphide marbles. For more complete information on these artisans, we refer you to our book *Contemporary Marbles* by Mark P. Block, published by Schiffer Publishing Ltd. in October 2000.

The most striking difference between antique and contemporary sulphide marbles is the clarity and sharpness of the contemporary vs. the antique marbles. The antique sulphides were made and used as toys. The contemporary marbles are made as works of art for collecting and decorative purposes.

Many contemporary glass artisans produce sulphide marbles, starting with Joseph St. Clair (deceased), who made a variety of subjects. Most of his work is signed.

Other craftsmen who produced or are producing sulphide marbles include:

Harry Besett
Harry & Kathleen Boyer
Buddy Buttler
Andy Davis
Jim Davis
Dudley Giberson
Charles Gibson
Steven Maslach
Boyd A. Miller
Ro Purser
Joe Rice
Joseph St. Clair (dec)

It should be noted that some of these artisans make their own sulphide figures, while others purchase them and case them in their own glass. Most of the contemporary artists use colored or white figures in clear glass and fire polish the pontil marks for a smooth, polished finish.

V-4-1. Painted Bird, 2 7/8". *Courtesy of Harry & Kathleen Boyer.*

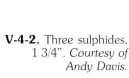

V-4-2. Three sulphides, 1 3/4". *Courtesy of Andy Davis.*

V-4-3. Painted Pig, 2". *Courtesy of Jim Davis.*

V-4-4. Painted Penguin, 2". *Courtesy of Jim Davis.*

V-4-5. Squirrel, 1 7/8". *Courtesy of Boyd A. Miller.*

V-4-6. Painted Owl, 1 7/8". *Courtesy of Boyd A. Miller and Tom Thornburgh.*

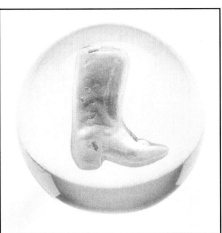

V-4-7. Boot, 1 3/4". *Courtesy of Steve Maslach.*

V-4-8. Teddy Bear, 1 7/8".
Courtesy of Prestige Glass.

V-4-9. Blue Bird, 1 7/8".
Courtesy of Prestige Glass.

V-4-10. Marble Shooter, on a separate 4" green glass base, 2 1/2".
Courtesy of Ro Purser.

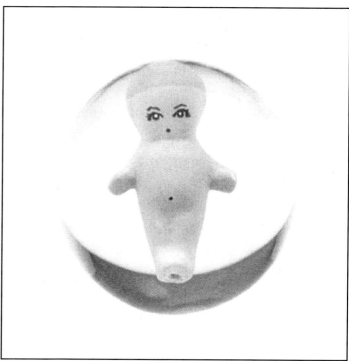

V-4-11. Sulphide Baby, 1 3/4". *Courtesy of Joe Rice.*

V-4-12. Hobby Horse, 1 3/4".
Courtesy of Joe Rice.

V-4-13. Bust of George Washington, from Presidential Series, 1 3/4". *Courtesy of Joe St. Clair (dec.).*

V-4-14. Turtle, painted figure, 1 3/4". *Courtesy of Joe St. Clair (dec.).*

V-4-15. Baseball Player, painted figure, 1 3/4". *Courtesy of Joe St. Clair (dec.).*

V-4-16. Reclining Elf, painted figure, 1 3/4". *Courtesy of Joe St. Clair (dec.).*

Glossary of Terms

This glossary of terms presents accepted definitions for marbles, related terms for sulphide marbles, and general terms used in the hobby of marbles.

Aggies: A common term used on the playgrounds of earlier times to refer to both glass and stone playing marbles of better quality or favored sort.

Alleys: Derived from alleytors; prized shooters made of semiprecious minerals. *See also* Aggies.

Anneal: The process of gradually reducing glass temperature, usually in an oven or lehr, for the purpose of balancing internal stresses throughout the glass and preventing fractures that would otherwise occur when the object reached room temperature.

Antique: According to United States customs laws: an item, usually a work of art, furniture, or decorative object made at least one hundred years ago. In the hobby of marbles, antique refers to marbles made prior to World War I.

Batch: Mixture of raw materials, properly proportioned and mixed, ready for use in the manufacture of glass. A typical mixture includes: (1) silica sand (the relatively pure quartz base material); (2) soda or potash to lower the melting point; (3) lime to harden and make the metal easier to work; (4) lead for brilliance; (5) borax for greater hardness; (6) metallic oxides to clear and color; and (7) cullet (broken glass) to lower the melting temperature of the batch.

Blown Glass: A glass object that is formed using blown air, as opposed to rolling, drawing, fusing, molding, etc. Marbles are not blown glass.

Bowling: (1) Rolling the shot, on the ground, to hit a marble. (2) Any of several games in which balls are rolled on an outdoor green, or down an indoor alley, at an object or group of objects.

Bruised: The condition of a marble that has received a visibly damaging blow, but no part has been chipped off. Sometimes bruising does not reduce the value quite as much as chips. *See also* Condition.

Bumboozer: A very large marble (1 inch and over) used as a bowling shooter. *See also* Hogger.

Chasies: Marble game, usually with two players. Players alternate shooting at each other's marble. Also known as "follow-up" (Midwest).

Chips: Pieces broken from the surface of a marble.

Clearie: A type of handmade or machine made marble of undecorated transparent glass.

Collectible (Poor): The worst marble condition expected in a collection. Badly damaged, but has some redeeming features. *See also* Condition.

Collector: One who gathers specimens for the purpose of study or ornament. Contrasts with "accumulator" in implying a more careful selection that leads to enjoyment of the aesthetic values pursued . . . and the knowledge gained and shared in fellowship.

Compatibility: The mutual characteristics of two or more batches of glass that allow them to be fused together and, after proper cooling, retain no stresses which will result in fractures. *See also* Anneal, Batch.

Condition and Grading: The grading of condition is very subjective. Every collector has their own opinion and no two collectors will likely agree on the exact condition of a particular marble. The Marble Collectors' Society of America uses a descriptive grading system (Mint, Near Mint, Good, Collectible), which allows for some flexibility in grading. A numerical grading system based on a scale of 1 to 10 has also developed among marble collectors. The description of each grading label used by the Society, along with the equivalent numerical grading is:

> **Mint:** A marble that is in original condition. The surface is unmarked and undamaged. There may be some minor rubbing on the surface; however, the marble is just the way it came from the factory. (10.0 – 9.0)

> **Near Mint:** A marble that has experienced minor usage. There may be evidence of some hit marks, usually tiny subsurface moons, pin prick chips, tiny flakes, or tiny bruises. The damage is inconsequential and does not detract from viewing the marble. If there is noticeable damage, and it is on only one side of the marble, the other side is considered Mint. (8.9 – 8.0)

Good: A marble that has experienced minor usage. It will have numerous hit marks, subsurface moons, chips, flakes, or bruises. The core can still be clearly seen, but the marble shows obvious use. If the damage is large or deep, and it is confined to one side, the other side is considered Mint or Near Mint. (7.9 – 7.0)

Collectible: A marble that has experienced significant usage, featuring overall moons, chips, flakes, and bruises. The core is completely obscured in some spots. A collectible marble has served its purpose and been well used. Still, it is a place holder in a collection until a better example replaces it. (6.9 – 0.0)

Any damage to the surface of a marble, no matter how slight, will affect its value. For a given amount of damage, the depreciation of value is much greater for machine made marbles than for handmade marbles. Even a small chip will effectively reduce the value of a machine made marble by more than half. Collectors tend to be more forgiving of damage to a handmade marble; the reason for this is probably directly related to the difficult in obtaining any handmade marbles.

The size of a marble is generally measured by its diameter in inches. Marble manufacturers utilize a sieve system of measuring. Using a device that measured marbles in 1/16 inch increments, the smallest opening that the marble would fall through was its size. Because of this method, the marbles classified as one size by a manufacturer could in fact vary by 3/64 inch. It was technically impossible to produce an antique handmade glass marble in sizes greater than approximately 2-1/2 inches in diameter because the marble would sag and deform during the annealing process due to its weight. This has changed with modern techniques and spheres as large as grapefruits can be made. However, different types of marbles are more common in some sizes than others. Machine made marbles are usually ½ inch to ¾ inch. This is because marble tournament regulations set the size of the shooters to be between ½ inch and ¾ inch and the size of the target marbles to be 5/8 inch. Again, the relative rarity of different sizes varies greatly from one type of marble to another.

Crystal: Clear, colorless glass; the body and case glass of most handmade marbles. Colorless as compared with colored transparent glass.

Cullet: Scraps of broken and waste glass to be remelted. Cullet added to the batch lowers the melting point of the raw material. *See also* Batch.

Diameter: The length of a straight line through the center of an object. The size of a marble is measured by its greatest diameter.

Ding: Minor damage to a marble caused by a blow, resulting in a small chip missing.

Donut Hole: Refers to holes as part of sulphide figures.

Excellent: An obscure term when referring to the condition of a marble. Mint is less subjective, and has been recognized to describe the best condition of a marble that remains undamaged but not in its original container. *See also* Mint, Condition.

Fire Polish: (1) The natural process gloss left on a marble by the heat used in manufacturing. (2) The polish resulting from subjecting a preheated marble to direct flame or radiant heat. Not a recommended procedure for novices.

For Fair: Marble play that ends with the return of all marbles won during the game to the former owner.

For Keeps: Marble play ending without the return of an opponent's marbles.

Fudging: Easing the hand over the ring line when in the act of shooting. Forbidden in tournament play. This term replaces "cheating" if the opponent is a big kid.

Furnace: Any of various ovens used for melting the glass batch. A kiln.

Gather: A portion of molten glass on a pontil. *See also* Metal, Punty, Pontil.

Glass: An amorphous (uncrystallized) substance consisting ordinarily of a silica (as sand), an alkali (as potash or soda), and some other alkali (as lime or lead oxide) fused together. Various colors are imparted by the addition of metallic oxides. *See also* Batch, Metal.

Glory Hole: An opening into the furnace or kiln used for reheating the gather of glass (the marble) when making a piece on a punty. *See also* Pontil.

Good: Third from best condition on a scale of four. *See also* Condition.

Ground: Refers to repairing a marble when considerable outer glass must be removed. If done by an expert, by hand, pontil marks may possibly be saved. When done on a sphere grinder, pontil marks are removed. When done in rock tumblers, the marble is usually ruined.

Handmade: Marbles made without use of machines, the exception being those held in the fingers against a power driven grinding wheel (e.g., agates made before 1910). Few handmade marbles of any sort can be expected to be perfect spheres; clay, pottery, and china types are the most out-of-round.

Histing: Raising the hand from the ground while in the act of shooting. Not allowed in tournament play. The cause of many blackened eyes.

Hogger: Any marble larger than 7/8 inch, and typically approximately 1 inch. Commonly, and misleadingly, called "shooter" size. Very few marbles were won with one of those big targets, as they are nearly impossible to shoot properly off the knuckle.

Hunching: Moving the hand forward while shooting over the ring line. Not allowed in tournament play. Also known as poking (Midwest).

Kabola: Oversized marble of jawbreaker size. *See also* Hogger.

Kiln: Any of various ovens, furnaces, used for the purpose of melting the glass batch, typically of brick construction, ceramic fiber lined, and, in the larger sizes, heated with natural gas. *See also* Lehr, Anneal.

Knuckles Down: To rest one or more of one's knuckles on the ground while shooting. A general term denoting the correct form for marble shooting. The marble should rest against the ball of the first finger rather than in the crook.

Lag: To pitch or shoot at a mark, marble, hole, or other target. In some areas (Midwest), pitch is distinguished from shoot. To pitch is to throw while shooting is to rest the marble on the first finger and to propel it with the thumbnail.

Lag Line: A straight line tangent to the ring in tournament play.

Lagging: The act of tossing or shooting from the pitching line. Whoever comes closest to the lag line, without going over it, shoots first.

Lehr: An oven in which glassware is annealed, typically fitted with a continuous belt feed. *See also* Anneal, Kiln.

Lofting: The act of shooting a marble through the air in an arc to hit another marble, or other target. Sometimes called popping.

Marble Shears: The tool used to hold, form, and cut a handmade marble as it is being made from the hot cane. Similar to tongs or sheep shears, but having a cup on one side and a blade on the other.

Marble Size: Antique glass marbles range in size from 1/2 inch to 2 1/2 inches. Contemporary marbles (spheres) can now be handmade as large as 6 inches in diameter.

Marbles: Marbles are little balls, made of hard substances (such as stone, glass, porcelain, clay, metal, etc.), and typically measuring from 5/8 inch to 2 1/2 inches in diameter. Decorative marbles range from as large as 6 inches to as small as ¼ inch.

Marver: Table on which hot glass is rolled. Originally made of marble, now of metal.

Metal: Molten (viscous) glass. *See also* Glass.

M.I.B.: The acronym for Mint-in-Box refers to original marbles, in their original box, in original condition. *See also* Condition, Mint, Near Mint.

MIBS: The game of marbles; represents shortening of the word marbles.

Mint: Established by long usage as the standard term meaning the original undamaged condition. *See also* Condition.

Near-Mint: Refers to the condition of a marble. Accepted by usage as next best grade. *See also* Condition.

Pitch Line: A straight line tangent to the ring, directly opposite and parallel to the lag line in the game of ringer. *See also* Lag Line.

Polishing: Removal of haze from the surface of a marble. When done properly, this process does not reduce the value of the marble and can greatly increase its beauty. Performed in a way (similar to grinding) where the polishing compound is applied to a cotton buffer.

Pontil: A long, solid steel rod. A device used to make the gather, to turn the gather while forming the marble, to finish, and to fire polish. Also called a punty. *See also* Punty.

Pontil Mark: A rough mark left on one or both poles of a handmade marble where the marble was sheared off the rod or the end of the punty. A cut off mark left on the marble.

Poor: Refers to condition of a marble. Marble has serious damage, chips, and/or cloudy surface. *See also* Condition.

Potsies: Name for the game of ringer. Also called dubs.

Punty: An iron or steel rod used to fashion hot glass which is attached by a rod of glass first gathered on the punty. Where detached from the glass, it leaves a rough spot.

Seed Bubbles: Tiny air bubbles in old glass. Seed bubbles may be deliberately placed in contemporary handmade marbles.

Seedy Glass: Glass containing many small gaseous inclusions (bubbles), usually introduced intentionally into base glass of both handmade and machine made marbles to create visual texture. *See also* Swirl Marbles.

Size: Usually measured with vernier calipers (brass or plastic), handmade marble size is the longest diameter. Machine made marbles are sized as follows:

7/16 inch	0000	1/16 inch	1	15/16 inch	5
½ inch	000	¾ inch	2	1 inch	6
9/16 inch	00	13/16 inch	3	1-1/16 inch	7
5/8 inch	0	7/8 inch	4	1-1/8 inch	8

Slip: (1) Misplay when marble falls from the hand. Player shoots over. (2) Player who drops the marble must call "slips" before Opponent calls "no slips" or loses the turn to shoot over (playgrounds in the Midwest). (3) The soupy mixture of clay used to cast sulfide figures. *See also* Sulphides.

Snooger: A near miss in a game of marbles.

Soda Lime Glass: Glass made from silica, soda, and lime. *See* Batch.

Spanners: A shooting distance. The measurement between the tip of the thumb to the tip of the middle finger when stretched apart.

Spheres: Round objects over 2 1/2 inches in diameter.

Stick: A shooter's marble (stops) inside the ring after knocking a target marble out of the ring. The player may continue to shoot as long as the shooter sticks inside the ring.

Stria: Elongated imperfections in glass. May be bubbles or may be caused by unequal density of glasses used. Stria cause variation in intensity of hues, as in stained glass windows. *See also* Batch, Anneal, Compatibility.

Sulphide Marbles: A type of handmade marble produced of transparent glass, and containing one or more sulphide (clay) figures of persons, animals, toys, numerals, or other objects. Sulphide marbles made of colored transparent glass with multiple figures or with painted sulphide objects occur. (Also spelled sulfide.)

Sulphides: Ceramic objects cast or molded of china clay and supersilicate of potash for inclusion in marbles and other glass ware. (Also spelled sulfide.)

Wet Mint: Referring to the condition of a marble. A Wet Mint look can be applied to the surface of a marble with a coating of liquid acrylic floor wax. *See also* Condition, Mint, Polish.

Bibliography

Allen, Shirley. *"Windy." The Game of Marbles.* Paden City, West Virginia: Marble King, Inc., 1953, revised 1967.

Armstrong, Joan. "She Wants All the Marbles." *News Gazette* (Champaign, Illinois), 19 Oct. 1981: A1, A5.

Avedon, Elliot M. and Brian Sutton-Smith (eds.). *The Study of Games.* New York: Wiley, 1971: "Folklore Source": 159-66(65). "Historical Sources": 121-27(22).

Baumann, Paul. *Collecting Antique Marbles.* Wallace Homestead Book Co., 1991.

Bergstrom, Evangeline H. *Old Glass Paperweights.* New York, Crown Publishers, 1940.

Block, Mark. *Contemporary Marbles.* Atglen, Pennsylvania: Schiffer Publishing, Ltd., 2000.

Block, Robert. *Marbles: Identification and Price Guide.* Atglen, Pennsylvania: Schiffer Publishing, Ltd., 1996, 1998.

Block, Stanley. *Marble Mania.* Atglen, Pennsylvania: Schiffer Publishing, Ltd., 1998.

Block, Stanley. "Marbles – Playing for Fun and For Keeps." *The Encyclopedia of Collectibles – Lalique to 7 degree Marbles.* Time-Life Publications, 1983.

Chestney, Linda. "Collectibles: Marbles." *New Hampshire Profiles*, April 1984: 29-32, 37, 48- 49 (30, 48).

Cloak, Evelyn Campbell. *Glass Paperweights of the Bergstrom Art Center.* New York, Crown Publishers, 1969.

Connor, Helen. "Professor's Hobby 'Marble-ous.'" *Indianapolis Star*, 3 January 1982, sec. 5:1-2.

Dunlop, Paul H. *The Jokelson Collection of Antique Cameo Incrustation.* Phoenix, Arizona, Papier Presse, 1991.

Garland, Robert. "That's Marbles, Son." *Saturday Evening Post,* 13 July 1946: 69.

Gold, Anita. "Antiques: Shows, Auctions, Clubs Come into Play for Toy Collectors." *Chicago Tribune,* 13 June 1986, sec 7: 53.

Hollister, Paul Jr. The Encyclopedia of Glass Paperweights. New York, Bramhall House, 1969.

Howe, Bea. "The Charm of Old Marbles." *Country Life,* 11 December 1969: 1593.

Huffer, Lloyd and Chris Huffer. "Marbles: Today's Game Is Collecting." *Antiques And The Arts Weekly,* 11 May 1990: 1, 108-10.

Jokelson, Paul. *Antique French Paperweights.* New York, Published Privately, 1955.

Jokelson, Paul. *Sulphides - The Art of Cameo Incrustation.* New York, Galahad Books, 1968.

Lidz, Franz. "Spotlight: Here's a Man Who Has All of His Marbles-Maybe Some of Yours, Too." *Sports Illustrated,* 3 December 1984: 7.

Louis, Sally B. "Playing for Keeps: Collecting Antique Marbles." *New York-Pennsylvania Collector,* December 1985: 1B-2B, 4B.

"Marble Society Produces Video." *American Collector's Journal,* September 1987: 4.

"Marbles." *New York Times Magazine,* 20 July 1914: 2.

"Marbles." *Saturday Review,* 26 July 1884: 107-08.

McClinton, Katherine Morrison. "Marbles." *Antiques Of American Childhood.* New York: Barmahall, 1970; 207-09.

Metzerott, Mary. "Notes on Marble History." *Hobbies,* November 1941: 56-57.

Randall, Mark E. and Dennis Webb. *Greenberg's Guide To Marbles.* Sykeville, Maryland: Greenberg, 1988.

Soble, Ronald L. "Your Collectibles: Losing His Marbles to Highest Bidder." *Los Angeles Times,* 20 March 1986, sec. 5: 20.

Steadham, Edward. "Enthusiast from Trumbull Shoots for World's Best Marble Collection." *Bridgeport Post,* 26 November 1983: 15.

Webb, Dennis. *Greenberg's Guide to Marbles.* Second Edition. Greenberg Publishing Co.: 1994.

Appendices
Appendix I: Marbles on Computer

By now, most have found themselves bombarded with today's technology revolution—news of the Internet, World Wide Web, cyberspace, the Information Superhighway, "going on-line," and "net-surfing." Marble collecting, and antiquing in general, using the Internet and on-line services is growing at a rapid pace. The Internet has provided collectors with a remarkable efficient means of communicating and exchanging information, as well as other previously non-traditional forms of buying and selling. There are a number of ways you can enhance your marble collecting experience by going "on-line."

Discussion Groups

By having conversations through computers with other marble collectors, you have another avenue to get your questions answered, buy and sell marbles and find out about shows and auctions, using one of the on-line service "message boards." You can also participate in the Marble Collectors Mailing List and bulletin board at www.marblecollecting.com. There are also small groups on CompuServe and Microsoft Network, as well as occasional postings in the UseNet Newsgroups.

The World Wide Web

The World Wide Web is the fastest growing area for on-line collecting. There is a tremendous wealth of information on the "Web," and more is being added each day. The largest and most comprehensive marble related web page is marblecollecting.com. This page links to the MCSA's web site www.marblemania.com; on-line version of the book *Marbles: Identification and Price Guide*; marble game instructions; marble show schedules; listing of marble clubs; auction information and links; Reproduction Alert page and classified ads. Collectors are creating more marble web sites seemingly every day. Marblecollecting.com has an up-to-date listing and links to numerous other marble web sites.

Cyber-Auctions

Aside from buying and selling marbles on the Web, you can also use the Internet to participate in marble auctions. Block's Box (www.blocksite.com) and Running Rabbit (www.runningrabbit.com) both accept valid bids via e-mail for their absentee auctions. There are always marbles listed on several general antique absentee auction web sites as well. Live marble auctions are also being held on-line now. A Chip Off The Old Block (www.blocksite.com) runs live marble auctions twice a week on the Internet.

Whether you want to connect with other marble collectors, locate information on marbles and marble collecting, or buy and sell marbles, "cyberspace" is fast becoming an essential element in your collecting repertoire.

Appendix II: Marble Shows

Shows and the dates they are held change each year. Listed here are the shows that were scheduled in 2000. It is best to call the show coordinators shown to verify future dates and locations.

Month	Name and Location	Contact for Information
January	Shawnee Marble Show Ullin, IL	Steven Johnson 618-833-3399
	Santa Cruz Marble Festival Santa Cruz, CA	Larry Van Dyke 702-656-1513
February	Buckeye Winterfest New Philadelphia, OH	Brenda Longbrake 419-642-5191 Steve Smith 330-364-8658
	Suncoast Marble Show St. Petersburg, FL	Catherine Kortvely 727-528-0699 Susan Tokarz 727-535-7870
March	Ozark Marble Show Springdale, AR	Taunya Kopke 501-582-0882
	Baltimore - Washington Show Perry Hall, MD	Joan Hayden 410-893-4929
	Sea - Tac Marble Show Seattle, WA	Larry Van Dyke 702-656-1513
April	Illinois Meet Ottawa, IL	Ron & Dee Hetzner 815-434-5698
	Texas Marble Collectors Garland, TX	Ron Roberts 214-352-8034
	Northboro Marble Show Northboro, MA	Carl Popp 508-842-7098
	Denver Marble Show Denver, CO	Larry Van Dyke 702-656-1513
	Pride of the Prairie Decatur, IL	Guy Gregg 217-795-4845
May	Maine Marble Meet S. Portland, ME	Mickie Pasenen 207-839-4726 Gary Stetson 207-657-4165
	West Virginia Marble Show Cairo, WV	Dean Six 304-643-2217
	Marble Show Wytheville, VA	Junior Stoots 540-236-2249
June	Marble Collectors Unlimited Amana Colonies, IA	Gary Huxford 319-642-3891
July	Marble Collectors Show Tulsa, OK	Neil or Debbie Thacker 918-322-9221
	Texas Marble Collectors Victoria, TX	Jerry Thompson 361-785-4303
	Golden Gate Marbles Show Millbrae, CA	Larry Van Dyke 702-656-1513
August	Buckeye Marble Collectors Columbus, OH	Brenda Longbrake 419-642-5191 Brian Estepp 614-863-5350
	Great Plains Marble Meet Council Bluffs, IA	Steve Campbell 712-527-9162
	Denver Marble Show Denver, CO	Larry Van Dyke 702-656-1513
September	Low Country Marble Show N. Charleston, SC	Mickey Gifford or James Gifford 843-835-8409
	Houston Marble Show Houston, TX	Woody Newman 281-493-0808
	Crossroads of America Show Kokomo, IN	Beth Morris 765-457-2477
	Mountain Home Show Mountain Home, AR	Ken Dunteman 870-424-7274
	Midwest Marble Club Bloomington, MN	Dorothy Vayder 612-831-3066
October	Northeast Marble Meet Marlborough, MA	Bert Cohen 617-247-4754
	Cincy Marble Show Cincinnati, OH	Cliff Himmler 513-232-4223
	Texas Marble Show New Braunfels, TX	John Tays 830-620-0217

	Smoky Hill Show Salina, KS	Larry Sawyer 785-472-3256
	Badger Marble Club Madison, WI	Bill Bass 608-723-6138
November	Las Vegas Show Las Vegas, NV	Larry Van Dyke 702-656-1513
December	Tom & Huck Show Hannibal, MO	John Miller 573-221-3900 Jack Noonan 573-588-7833

Appendix III: Marble Clubs

Following is a current listing of marble clubs.

Akro Agate Collector's Club
Roger Hardy
10 Bailey St.
Clarksburg, WV 26301

Badger Marble Club
Jim Stephenson
PO Box 194
Waunakee, WI 53597
Show

Blue Ridge Marble Club
Roger Dowdy
2401 Brookmont Court
Richmond, VA 23233
Show, Newsletter

Buckeye Marble Collectors
Brenda Longbrake
PO Box 3051
Elida, OH 45807
Shows, Newsletter

Canadian Marble Collectors Association
59 Mill St.
Milton, Ontario, Canada L9T JR8
Newsletters

Great Plains Marble Club
c/o Steve Campbell
508 Sixth St.
Glenwood, IA 51534
Show

Indiana Marble Club
Beth Morris
765-457-2477
Show

Knuckledown Marble Club
Daniel Ambrose
3112 Amherst Rd.
Erie, PA 16506

Maine Marble Club
Micki Pasanen
47 Burnham Rd.
Gorham, ME 04038
Show

Marble Collectors' Society of America
Stanley Block
PO Box 222
Trumbull, CT 06611
Newsletter, Books, Videos, Other Publications

Marble Collectors Unlimited
Beverly Brule
PO Box 201
Northboro, MA 05132
Show, Newsletter

Midwest Marble Club
Kenneth Royer, Treasurer
3 Mallard Lane
St. Paul, MN 55127
Show, Newsletter

Oklahoma Marble Collectors
c/o Neil or Debbie Thacker
16328 South Peoria
Bikby, OK 74008
Shows

Sea-Tac Marble Club
Larry Van Dyke
PO Box 336111
North Las Vegas, NV 89031
Shows, Newsletter

South Jersey Marble Collectors
Joseph C. Brauner, Jr.
7709 Raymond Dr.
Millville, NJ 08322

Southern California Marble Collectors Society
Sherry Ellis
PO Box 6913
San Pedro, CA 90734
Show

Sun Coast Marble Collectors Society
Catherine Kortvely
PO Box 60213
St. Petersburg, FL 22784
Show, Newsletter

Texas Marble Collectors
John W. Tays
417 Marsh Oval
New Braunfels, TX 78130
Shows, Meeting

Tri-State Marble Collectors Club
David French
PO Box 18924
Fairfield, OH 45018
Show

Index

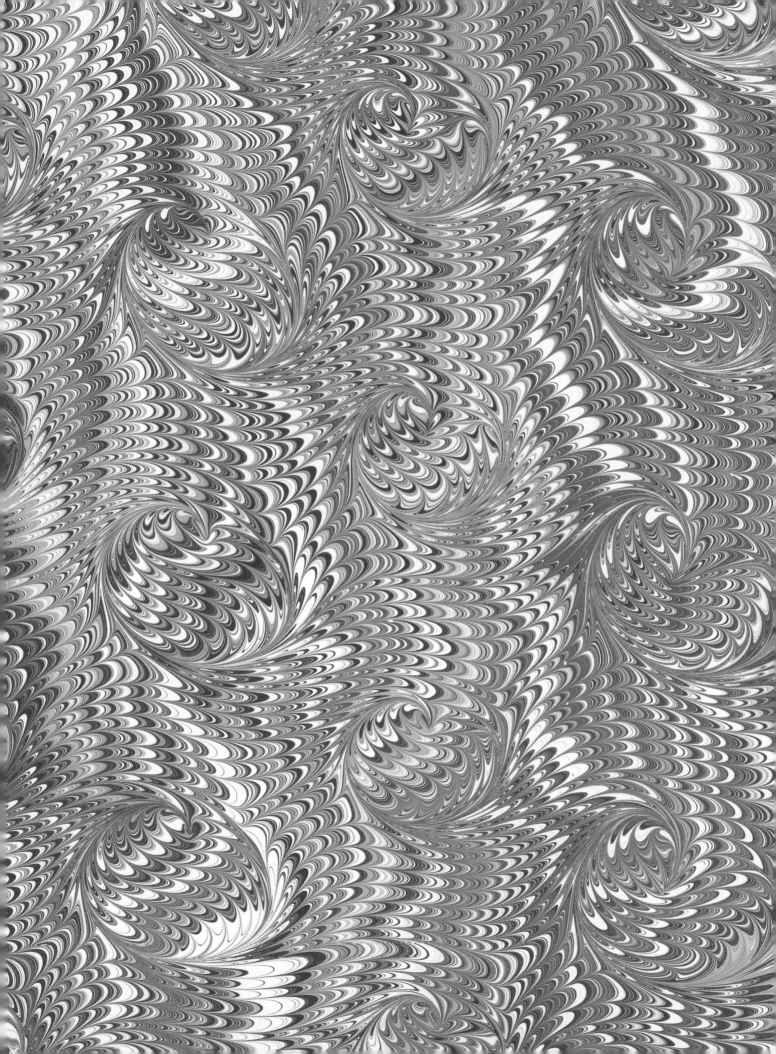